The Doubleday
Children's Picture Dictionary

The Doubleday
Children's
Picture
Dictionary

Compiled by Felicia Law • Illustrated by Carol Holmes

Doubleday & Company, Inc.
Garden City, New York

Library of Congress Cataloging-in-Publication Data

Law, Felicia.
    The Doubleday children's picture dictionary.

    Summary: An illustrated beginner dictionary providing
simple definitions for over 1500 entries. Includes a
pronunciation guide, spelling checklist, and maps.
    1. English language — Dictionaries, Juvenile.
[1. English language — Dictionaries] I. Holmes,
Carol, ill. II. Doubleday and Company, Inc.
III. Title.
PE1628.5.L38   1987   423   86-16216
ISBN 0-385-23711-1

English–The Language We Speak

"Hello! Good Day! I am American and I speak English. My friends are also saying 'Hello! Good Day!' to you, but not in English. They are saying it in their own languages – in German, in French, in Swahili, in Italian, in Japanese, and in Arabic."

Did you know that there are over 3,000 languages in the world? Chinese is spoken by more people than any other language. But it is only really spoken in China – and there are more than a billion Chinese. But English is spoken in many more places all over the world than any other language. It is spoken by one out of every eight people. Besides being the main language in the United States and Canada (except in Quebec), it is the national language of Australia, New Zealand, and many countries of Africa. It is also spoken in many islands of the West Indies, in India, Pakistan, Bangladesh, and Sri Lanka and in Ireland. And of course English is the national language of England, the country from which English gets its name.

The English that is spoken in the British Isles – British English – is slightly different from American English or Australian English. The English, Irish, Scots, and Welsh each pronounce words in their own way. They also have different names for things. What we in America call an elevator the British call a lift. We put gasoline in our automobiles while the British put petrol in their cars. Americans

People all over the world speak many different languages.

Hello

Guten tag

Bon jour

Jambo

Buon giorno

こんにちは

أَهْلاً وَسَهْلاً

live in apartments, the British live in flats; Americans eat candy, the British eat sweets; Americans travel on subways and railroads, the British travel on the underground and the railways.

English is an amazingly rich language. It has borrowed words from many other languages. When the French-speaking Normans conquered England in 1066, they gave English many new words. For instance the English sheep became French mutton when it was served on the Norman rulers' tables. In the same way pigs became pork. When English-speaking people went to America in the early 1600s, they borrowed many words from the American Indians to describe things for which they had no English name. Examples of such words are tomahawk, canoe, and moose.

These people lived over 30,000 years ago. They hunted animals with spears and made their homes in caves. On the walls of the caves they painted pictures of horses, reindeer, and bison. Perhaps this was an early kind of writing.

First language

We do not know when people first began using words. Perhaps at first people used a kind of sign language to say what they wanted. Later they might have invented sounds for things, simple words. And in different places people used different sounds for the same thing. In this way perhaps language developed.

At first people learned all the words they knew by hearing them – just as very small children do now. It was only very much later that people learned how to write. This was mainly in order to keep records of what they had bought or sold.

At first people would just draw a picture of a thing they wanted to record – a man, a woman, an ox, a bird. The people of Ancient Egypt could write quite complicated messages using kinds of pictures. The people of Ancient China also drew pictures of the things they wanted to write about. In time these pictures became much simpler – just a few brush strokes. They became known as characters. Chinese is still written in characters to this day.

A long time ago – over 3,000 years – a new way of writing was developed. Instead of pictures it used different signs for each sound in a word. A letter stood for a sound. We call letters which stand for sounds an alphabet. There are several different kinds of alphabet. The alphabet we use for writing down English has 26 letters. They are:

Aa Bb Cc Dd Ee Ff Gg Hh Ii Jj Kk Ll Mm Nn Oo Pp Qq Rr Ss Tt Uu Vv Ww Xx Yy Zz

These are the bricks we use to build words. In the English language there are nearly half a million words, far more than any other language. Yet the English Bible uses only about 7,000 of these words. In ordinary life few people use more than 1,500 to 3,000 words. Your *Doubleday Children's Picture Dictionary* will tell you about 1,500 of these English words. We hope you will want to learn more about our language.

friend   buffalo

tepee   peace

horse   trade

In North America when one tribe spoke to another tribe, they used sign language.

The Chinese write with "characters." Their writing is written downward. The characters are painted with a brush.

Different kinds of alphabet. From top to bottom they are: Our alphabet; the Russian alphabet; the Japanese alphabet; and the Greek and Arabic alphabets.

How To Use Your Dictionary

We hope that your *Doubleday Children's Picture Dictionary* will help you to learn a lot about words. That is what a dictionary is really for – to explain what words mean and to show you how to spell them.

Before you start using this book, we should like to tell a little about how it works. This way you will get a lot more out of it.

Like all dictionaries, this dictionary contains a long list of words – over 1,500. To make it easier for you to look them up, the words are all put into the ABC order of the letters of the alphabet. You must of course know the ABC. You will remember that it goes like this (in BIG capital letters followed by small letters):

Aa Bb Cc Dd Ee Ff Gg Hh Ii Jj Kk Ll Mm Nn Oo Pp Qq Rr Ss Tt Uu Vv Ww Xx Yy Zz

In this dictionary all the words beginning with the letter A – **abacus, about, above, abroad** and so on, are all put together. These are followed by all the words beginning with B (**baboon, baby, back**...), and those beginning with C and so on all the way through to the letter Z – **zebra, zero, zigzag, zipper,** and **zoo,** the very last word in the dictionary.

So which comes first, **panda** or **mouse**? Easy. The letter M comes before the letter P in the alphabet. So **mouse** must come before **panda**.

Now which comes first, **helmet** or **hat**? Both words begin with H, so you have to look at the second letter of each word – e in helmet and a in hat. The a in hat comes

An early typewriter.

8

before the e in helmet, so hat comes before helmet. Can you work out why **lion** comes before **lip**?

Black Words

To make it easier to find the words you want to look up, we have printed these words in heavy black letters like this: **horse**.

Under each word in heavy black letters that you look up you will find out what the word means. Suppose you chose the word **acorn**. On the next line you will be told that "An **acorn** is the nut of the oak tree." This is followed by a sentence: "Big oaks grow from little **acorns**." This gives us another form of the word acorn – with an "s" at the end, which we use when we want to talk about more than one acorn. Just suppose you don't know what the word "nut" means. Look that word up and you will discover that "A **nut** is a hard shell with a fruit or seed inside." And if you don't know what an **oak** is look that up too. You will learn that "An **oak** is a tall wide-spreading tree." Whenever the word you are looking up is repeated in either the same or in a different form in the "definition," it is printed in heavy black letters. Here is a good example:

collect

When you bring things together you **collect** them. I am **collecting** stamps from all over the world. Have you seen his **collection** of foreign coins?

You will see that all the different forms of **collect** are printed in thicker letters.

You will notice that many words in this dictionary have a sentence to help you understand the meaning. This shows the words "at work." Here is an example:

behind

The place at the back of something or someone is **behind**. Peter stood **behind** Joe in the line. There is a large garden **behind** the wall.

How to speak words

You may not know how to say some of the words. You can't "pronounce" them. Do you know how to say know?!! No! How do you say knot? Maybe you would rather not!

Well after the headword (the word you want to look up, which is printed in heavy type) you will sometimes see a "pronunciation guide." This tells you how to speak the word. So after the word **ache**, for instance, you will see (ake). This tells you that **ache** is said like "ake." And **know** is said like "no," and **knot** is said like "not." (As if you didn't already know!)

There are some words which are spelled the same but which have quite different meanings. Take for instance the word **light**. Look the word up in this dictionary and you will see that it has two meanings. The first meaning (following the number 1) is what is given off by the sun and by lamps. The second meaning (following the number 2) is "not heavy."

The Spelling Checklist

At the end of this dictionary there is a list of words which you may want to spell. There are about 3,000 of them and they are all in alphabetical order. No meanings – or definitions – are given. But many of the words also appear in the main part of your dictionary where meanings are given. So if you are not quite sure how to spell a word – say ceiling, or handkerchief, or height, or library – look it up in the spelling checklist.

We hope you will enjoy this dictionary, use it a lot, and learn more and more about our language.

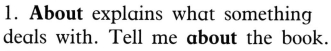

A a

A is used a lot in talking and writing. It is often used before the name of a thing. We say "**a** ball can bounce," or "I saw **a** bird fly."

abacus

A frame with beads that move on rods is called an **abacus**. You can add, subtract, multiply, or divide with an **abacus**. In China, people have counted with an **abacus** for thousands of years.

An **abacus** can be used to add, subtract, multiply, and divide.

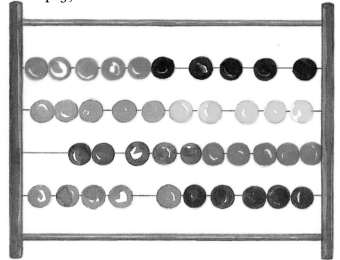

about

1. **About** explains what something deals with. Tell me **about** the book. 2. It can also mean roughly or more or less. John ate **about** fifteen chocolates.

above

Above describes the space overhead. The sky **above** is bright blue. The aircraft flew **above** the trees.

abroad

You will be **abroad** if you are in a foreign country. Do you go **abroad** for your vacation?

absent

To be **absent** means to be away, or not to be there. John was **absent** from school when he was sick.

accept

To **accept** means to take what is given to you. The winner **accepted** a prize from the judge.

accident (ax-id-ent)
An **accident** is usually unexpected and unpleasant. The dog ran across the traffic and caused a terrible **accident**.

across
The dog dashed **across** the road. It ran from one side to the other.

The dog ran through the traffic and caused a terrible **accident**.

ache (ake)
Something **aches** when the pain goes on and on. When your tooth is **aching**, you go to the dentist.

acorn
An **acorn** is the nut of an oak tree. Big oaks grow from little **acorns**.

act
1. When people perform on the stage, they are **acting**. Actors and actresses **act** at the theater.
2. An **act** is a deed. The boy scout did his good deed for the day. It was an **act** of bravery.

add
If you want to find how many things you have, you must **add** them up. One **added** to two equals three. Can you **add** these numbers: $4 + 5 + 4 = ?$

acrobat
An **acrobat** does gymnastic feats. At the circus we saw three **acrobats** balanced on a ball.

Acrobats must be good at balancing.

address
Your **address** on a letter tells the mailman where you live. Always write the **address** clearly on the envelope.

11

admire
We think well of people or things we **admire**. We **admire** brave firefighters who do dangerous work.

adult
An **adult** is a grown-up. "Come to the circus: **Adults** allowed in only if accompanied by a child!"

advance
The general told the army to **advance** to the city of Moscow. **Advance** means to move forward.

adventure
An **adventure** is when something exciting happens. The great explorers had lots of **adventures**.

advertisement
An **advertisement** is a message about something for sale. Some people believe everything they see in **advertisements**. Goods for sale are **advertised** in newspapers and on TV.

aerial
An **aerial** is a metal rod that picks up signals from the air. Television signals are picked up by an **aerial**.

afford
If you have enough money, you can **afford** to buy things. How can you **afford** such an expensive car?

afraid
I am **afraid** of things that frighten me. I'm **afraid** of spiders and things that go bump in the night.

after
1. **After** can mean following behind. Jill won the race; Jack came **after**.
2. It can also mean later on. Come and see me **after** breakfast.

Cindy tried to frighten Ellen by showing her a spider. Is Ellen **afraid** of spiders?

afternoon
The part of the day between morning and evening is called the **afternoon**. Let's take a picnic and spend the **afternoon** on the beach.

again
If you do something once more, you are doing it **again**. We may have lost the game this time, but we'll try **again**.

age

1. Your **age** tells how many years you have lived. I am **aged** eight.
2. A period of history can be called an **Age**. Would you like to have lived in the Stone **Age**?

ago

Things that happened in the past happened some time **ago**. A few moments **ago** I was not sure what **ago** meant!

Would you rather have lived in the Stone **Age** or the Space **Age**?

agree

If you think the same as I do, you **agree** with me. We all **agree** that the earth is round.

ahead

Ahead means in front. I'll go **ahead** and get home before you.

aim

To **aim** means to point at. The policeman **aimed** his gun at the bank robber so he wouldn't run away.

air

We breathe in a gas called **air**. Why can't I fly through the **air** like a bird? **Air** is all around us.

airplane

A flying machine driven by a pilot is called an **airplane**. Airplanes land and take off from an airport.

Air is all around us. I wish I could fly through the **air** like a bird.

13

airport

An **airport** is a place where aircraft land and take off.

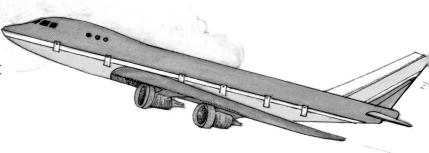

alarm

An **alarm** sounds as a signal to tell us of danger. When robbers entered the bank, the **alarm** went off.

Airplanes take off and land at **airports**.

album

1. An **album** is a book in which photos or stamps can be placed.
2. A record **album** is a long-playing record with many songs.

alike

Two things that look the same are said to be **alike**. Those two children are as **alike** as two peas in a pod.

alive

All living things, such as plants and animals, are **alive**. If they are not **alive** they are dead.

The **alligator** is looking **along** the tightrope at the acrobat.

all

All means everyone, everything or every part of something. "**All** the king's horses and **all** the king's men..."

alligator

An **alligator** is an animal that is covered with hard scales. It is a reptile that lives in the water and on land near water.

allow

If your mother lets you do something, she **allows** you to do it. Are you **allowed** to stay up late on school nights?

almost

Almost means very nearly. A baby leopon is **almost** a leopard and **almost** a lion. It's very mixed up!

along

The acrobat walked **along** the tightrope. She walked from one end to the other.

The acrobat is walking **along** the tightrope.

aloud

Read this sentence **aloud** so that everyone can hear. Read it out **loud**.

alphabet (al-fa-bet)

Our **alphabet** starts with a and ends with z. There are twenty-six letters altogether and each one stands for a different sound.

A B C D E
F G H I J
K L M N O
P Q R S T
U V W X Y
Z

You can see **almost** all the letters of the **alphabet**. Which letter can't you see?

already

Don't keep telling me to clean up my bedroom. I've **already** done it. I did it before.

also

I have a pet cat, **also** a dog, and a rabbit. **Also** means as well.

altogether

Altogether means entirely. The traffic warden was **altogether** right when she said to look both ways before crossing a street.

15

always

Always means the same as all the time. There are **always** leaves on an evergreen tree.

amaze

This magician will **amaze** the children with his tricks. Isn't he **amazing**! Isn't he surprising!

ambulance

An **ambulance** rushes sick or injured people to the hospital. It drives very fast through the traffic.

American

An **American** was born or lives in the United States of **America**. He or she is an **American** citizen.

We are all **Americans.**

amount

The **amount** of pocket money I get is never enough. The **amount** is the total sum.

amuse

We usually smile or laugh at things that **amuse** us. Clowns are very **amusing.**

an

An is used before a word instead of **a** when the word begins with a,e,i,o,u. I eat **an** apple and cook **an** egg.

anchor (ank-er)

A heavy piece of hooked metal called an **anchor** is thrown over the side of a boat to hold the boat in place. Many boats are **anchored** in the harbor.

and

And is a joining word. Two **and** two make four. He is tall **and** thin.

Angel

angel

An **angel** is a messenger from God. **Angels** brought news of Jesus' birth to the shepherds.

angry

Angry means feeling cross. John was **angry** when his sister sat on his doughnut.

animal

An **animal** is a living creature that can move and feel. Elephants, bees, and whales are all **animals**. Living things that are not **animals** are plants.

ankle

The joint between my foot and my leg is my **ankle**. Take care not to twist your **ankle**!

announce

To **announce** means to tell some news. "I have an **announcement** to make," said the radio **announcer**. He had some news to tell everyone.

annoy

If you **annoy** someone, you make them cross and angry. Mosquitoes are very `**annoying** on a warm summer's night.

another

Another means one more. Sing me **another** song.

answer (an-sur)

All questions need an **answer**. You must reply to them.

ant

An **ant** is a tiny insect. **Ants** live together in large groups called colonies.

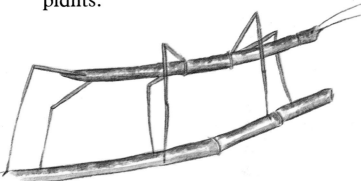

Can you see the stick insect? It is an **animal**, but it looks like a plant. **Ants** are tiny animals.

any

Have you **any** money? Have you some money? **Any** often means the same as some.

anyone

"Is **anyone** at home?" **Anyone** may be any person at all. You can also call out "Is **anybody** at home?"

anything

Do you have **anything** in your bag? Is it empty or is there something in it?

apart

1. Two houses may be streets **apart**. They are distant from each other.
2. When things grow old, they often fall to pieces. Poor old scarecrow, he's falling **apart**.

Apes have long **arms**. This one holds an **apple**.

The poor old scarecrow is falling to pieces. He's falling **apart**.

ape

A chimpanzee is an **ape**. **Apes** belong to the same family as monkeys, but they have no tails.

apologize

Sometimes it's not easy to **apologize** for doing something wrong. I'm very sorry! This is an **apology**.

appear

The ghost will **appear** at midnight. When it **appears**, it comes into sight.

appetite

The runners had built up a healthy **appetite** by the time they reached the finishing line. Your **appetite** gets stronger when you are hungry.

apple

Apples are the fruit of the **apple** tree. **Apple** pie is a great treat.

April

April is the fourth month of the year. **April** has thirty days.

apron

It is best to protect your clothing with an **apron** when you are cooking. A cook's **apron** gets very messy!

My aunt and I are making **apple** pies. We are wearing **aprons** to keep our clothes clean.

arch

An **arch** is a curved shape that is built to hold a lot of weight. **Arches** hold up bridges and churches.

architect (are-ki-tekt)

An **architect** plans the shape of buildings. **Architects** draw up plans for builders.

are

You **are** a girl. I am a boy. She is a doctor.

area

The **area** is the size of a surface. It is measured by the length and width of the space. My garden covers an **area** of one hundred square yards.

arena

An **arena** is a special place where sports events are held. The Olympic teams paraded in the **arena**.

argue

People sometimes **argue** when they disagree. The children **argued** over who should eat the last bun. They are always **arguing**. Who started the **argument** on the football field?

arm

The part of the body between the shoulder and the hand is called the **arm**.

The **arrows** can't harm this soldier! He is wearing a suit of **armor**.

armor

In olden days, soldiers wore a strong metal covering over the body to protect them in battle. This suit of metal is called **armor**.

army

A large group of soldiers is called an **army**. The **armies** marched up the hill and down again.

around

There was water all **around**. It was on all sides. The girl wore a belt **around** her waist.

arrange

To **arrange** something means to put it in order. My mother is **arranging** flowers in a bowl. Who **arranged** this Halloween party?

arrest

The police officer will **arrest** the burglar who is inside the bank. Someone who has done something wrong can be **arrested**.

arrive

When you reach a place you **arrive**. Tom **arrived** home late last night. The train **arriving** at platform one is the express from New York.

arrow

An **arrow** is a thin stick with a point at one end. It is shot from a bow. An archer uses a bow and **arrow**.

artist

A person who draws or paints is an **artist**. **Artists** make works of art.

Annie is painting a picture. She is an **artist**.

as

Jim is **as** tall **as** Mike. He is not taller and he is not shorter. Jane went to the party **as** a clown. She went dressed like a clown.

ash

1. The powder that is left when something burns is called **ash**. When the fire dies, the **ashes** will become cold.
2. **Ash** is the name of a tree. The **ash** tree has a hard wood.

An **ash** is a kind of tree.

ashamed

If you behave badly you sometimes feel guilty afterward. You feel guilty or **ashamed**.

ask

1. To **ask** means to put a question about something. The driver **asked** the way to the bus station.
2. To **ask** can also mean to request. How many times must I **ask** you to shut the door?

asleep

The baby is sleeping. She is **asleep**. She will be awake when she stops sleeping.

Astronauts travel in space.

astronaut

A person who travels in space is an **astronaut**. Three **astronauts** flew to the moon in a rocket.

at

At can mark the time or the place. I will meet you **at** the fountain **at** three o'clock.

athlete

An **athlete** is good at sports. We practice **athletics** at school.

atlas

An **atlas** is a book of maps. You can see where Moscow is in an **atlas.**

atmosphere (at-moss-fear)

The air around our earth is called the **atmosphere**. Airplanes travel through the **atmosphere** as they fly from place to place.

attack

The dog **attacked** the cat. They began to fight. Soldiers are trained to **attack** the enemy.

attention

To pay **attention** means to watch and listen carefully. Some children always pay **attention** in class.

August

August is the eighth month of the year. **August** has thirty-one days.

aunt

My mother's sister and my father's sister are my **aunts**. My **aunt** is married to my uncle.

autumn

Autumn is the season of the year

These **athletes** are running in a race.

that follows summer. Plants begin to die and lose their leaves in **autumn**

avenue

An **avenue** is a wide street. Trees sometimes grow on the sides of **avenues**.

awake

I am **awake** when I am not sleeping. Owls stay **awake** all night to hunt for food.

away

Take this empty dish **away**. Take it some distance from this place. If you go **away** you travel or leave.

ax

An **ax** is used for cutting down trees. It is a tool with a wooden handle and a sharp metal edge.

Bb

Baboon

baboon

A **baboon** is a large kind of monkey. We see **baboons** at the zoo. **Baboons** live in Africa.

baby

A **baby** is a young child. How can such tiny **babies** have such big voices?

back

The **back** of something is opposite to the front. You cannot see your own **back**. Mommy **backed** up her car. I sit at the **back** of the class.

backward

When you move **backward**, you move toward the back. You are not going forward. I am swinging **backward** and forward.

bacon

The meat from a pig is called **bacon** when it has been smoked or salted. I eat **bacon** and eggs for breakfast.

bad

Something that is **bad** is not good. I had a **bad** dream which frightened me. Jim plays the flute **badly**.

badge

A **badge** is a small sign with words or pictures worn by members of the same team or group. The sherriff wears a shiny **badge** on his jacket.

I wear a lot of **badges** on my sweater.

23

bag

A **bag** is a kind of sack to put things in. These **bags** are full of groceries from the store.

bake

To **bake** is to cook food in an oven. The **baker bakes** bread and cakes.

balance

The seal **balanced** the ball on its nose. It kept the ball steady in one place.

Look at the seal! It is **balancing** the **ball** on its nose.

bald

A **bald** man has little or no hair on his head. Pop is so **bald** his head looks like an egg.

ball

A **ball** is a round object. An orange is shaped like a **ball**. Can you throw the **ball** over the net?

ballet (bal-ay)

The **ballerina** danced on her toes in the **ballet** *Swan Lake*. **Ballet** is a kind of dance. Ballets usually tell a story.

balloon

Balloons float in the air. A bag filled with gas or air makes a **balloon**. We blew up rubber **balloons** and burst them with a pin.

banana

A **banana** is a long fruit which turns yellow when it is ripe. **Bananas** grow in clumps on a **banana** tree.

band

1. A **band** is a thin circle of cloth that holds things together. Suzy keeps her hair off her face with a **hairband**. I hold mine back with a rubber **band**.

2. A group of musicians can form a **band**. The brass **band** played a march.

bandage

A strip of material that is put over a cut is called a **bandage**. When Harry cut his knee, the doctor **bandaged** it up.

bang

He **banged** the table with his fist. He hit it violently and loudly. Let's start **banging** on the big bass drum, bing, bong, **bang**.

bank

1. Money is kept in a **bank**. Wild Jim robbed the Nabsville **Bank** in broad daylight.
2. Wild flowers grow on the river **bank**. The **bank** is a raised piece of ground.

The robber takes the money from the **bank**. The dog **barks**.

bar

A **bar** is a long piece of strong wood or metal. The horse jumped over a five-**bar** gate.

barbecue

In summer we invite our friends to a **barbecue**. We hold an outdoor party and cook the food on an open fire.

barber

A **barber** is someone who cuts men's or boys' hair.

bark

1. "Hark, hark, the dogs do **bark**." Dogs make a sharp cry called a **bark**.

2. **Bark** is the outer covering or skin of a tree. We made **bark** rubbings in the park using a black crayon and paper.

barn

A **barn** is a building on a farm. The farmer stores hay, grain, and other crops in **barns**.

My brother is splashing in the **bath.**

base

The bottom of something is its **base.** The lamp has a wooden **base.**

baseball

Baseball is a game played by two teams. Points are scored when the striker hits the ball with a bat and manages to score runs.

A **bat** is a furry animal with wings.

basement

The **basement** is the lowest room of a building. The furnace that heats our house is in the basement.

basket

A **basket** is a holder made of straw or other material. Fill the shopping **basket** with food.

basketball

Two teams of athletes play **basketball.** They throw a ball through a high hoop to score.

bat

1. A **bat** is a mouselike animal that can fly.
2. A **bat** is also a wooden stick used to play baseball.

bath

You can wash your whole body in a **bath**tub. We splash so much in the **bath** that half the water ends up on the floor.

be

This is an important word. It follows the name of a person or thing, and this causes it to change. I have promised to **be** good today. I **am being** good all day. I **am** not as fat as he **is,** but they **are** even fatter! The word **be** also changes to show when something happened. I **was** naughty yesterday, John **was** naughty too, but the twins **were** even naughtier. It **is** sunny today, but yesterday it **was** raining. "Pussy cat, pussy cat, where have you **been**?"

beach

The land on the seashore is called the **beach.** Some **beaches** are sandy.

beak

Birds use their **beaks** to peck or tear at their food. The **beak** is the hard, pointed part of a bird's mouth. The **beak** is an eating tool, so you can tell what a bird eats by the shape of its **beak**.

These birds all have different **beaks**.

Pelican

Hen

Parrot

Oystercatcher

bean

A **bean** is a vegetable with a large seed that can be cooked and eaten. There are many different kinds of **beans**, like kidney **beans** and broad **beans**; coffee **beans** and cacao **beans**.

The polar **bear** lives near the North Pole. It is white so that it can hide in the ice and snow.

bear

Bears are large, wild, furry animals. Polar **bears** live in Arctic regions. Grizzly **bears** live in North America.

beard

The hair that grows on a man's chin and cheeks is called a **beard**. In fairy tales, dwarfs have long white **beards**.

beat

1. To **beat** means to hit again and again. People used to **beat** their carpets to get the dust out.
2. When you win a race you **beat** the other competitors. Sid was **beaten** by Bert at their game of cards.

beautiful

Beautiful things please us when we look at them or listen to them. Music can be **beautiful** to listen to. It's a **beautiful** day!

Beavers build a home of mud and sticks.

beaver
A **beaver** is a furry animal with a long flat tail. It lives partly on land and partly in the water. **Beavers** build dams to block streams.

because
I can't dance **because** I've broken my leg. I can't dance for that reason.

become
When you **become** something, you grow to be it. Dick hopes to **become** a magician when he grows up. As the sun rose, the garden **became** full of light. It is **becoming** dark, so let's close the curtains.

bed
We sleep on a **bed** at night. At **bedtime** I go to **bed** in my **bedroom**.

I go to **bed** at eight o'clock.

bee
A **bee** is an insect which makes honey. It can also sting. People keep **bees** in a **beehive**.

beef
Beef is the meat from cattle. You can cook **beef** in a casserole or in a pie.

A **bee** is an insect. So is a **beetle**.

beetle
The **beetle** is an insect. Like all insects, it has six legs. A shell-like coat covers its wings and protects them.

before
Before can mean in front of. Jack stood **before** the giant's castle. **Before** also means earlier. The giant had locked the gate **before** Jack got there.

begin
When we **begin**, we start to do the first part of something. We **begin** to read a book on the first page. It is the **beginning** of the show. The cat **began** to chase the bird. Have you **begun** your homework yet?

behave

The way we act is the way we **behave**. Our dog **behaves** well. It sits when we tell it.

behind

The place at the back of something or someone is **behind**. Peter stood **behind** Joe in the line. There is a large garden **behind** that wall.

believe

Do you **believe** in Santa Claus? Do you think there is any truth in that story? Mike **believed** everything his father told him.

bell

A **bell** is a hollow object of metal. A small hammer hangs inside. When the hammer strikes the **bell**, you hear a musical sound.

belong

This book **belongs** to me. It is mine. I own it.

below

Below means underneath. He jumped from the window to the ground **below**. A sailor went **below** deck.

belt

A **belt** is a strip of material that you wear around your waist.

bend

A **bend** is another word for a curve. Some people have the power to **bend** forks. Dick **bent** over to look at the worm.

berry

A fruit with lots of seeds in it is called a **berry**. We eat **strawberries** and **blackberries**. There are **berries** we should never eat, such as mistletoe **berries**.

A **berry** is a small fruit with lots of seeds. Some **berries** must NOT be eaten.

beside

The old woman sat **beside** the fire. She sat at the side of it.

best

I wear my **best** clothes to parties. Jane is **better** than Joe at remembering things. The **best** is **better** than all the rest.

between

Between is the place in the middle of two things. The table is **between** two chairs. I go to school **between** eight o'clock and eight-thirty.

Bible

The **Bible** is a book that tells us stories about God. It was written a long time ago.

bicycle

A **bicycle** has two wheels. It is pushed along when the rider turns the pedals. My **bike** has a big bell.

I had a **blue bicycle** with **black** tires for my **birthday**.

The elephant is **between** the bars of the cage. Look! It's too **big**!

big

Big is large. The elephant was too **big** to go in the cage. The cat is **bigger** than the mouse. The **biggest** tree I ever saw was a redwood.

bill

1. The **bill** shows how much money you must pay when you buy something. Don't forget to pay the electricity **bill**!
2. A **bill** is another word for a bird's beak.

bird

Animals that are covered with feathers are called **birds**. All **birds** have wings and most of them use their wings to fly.

birth

The day of your **birth** is the day you leave your mother's body. When were you **born**?

30

birthday
The day on which you were born is your **birthday**. You enjoy your **birthday** each year.

bite
You use your teeth to **bite**, or to cut into things. Our silly dog **bit** its own tail. Let me see where it has **bitten** itself.

black
The darkest of all the colors is **black**. A chessboard has **black** and white squares.

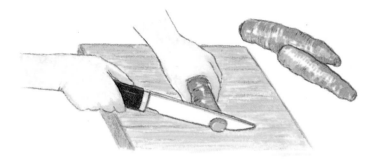

The **blade** of the knife cuts easily. It is not **blunt**. It is sharp.

blade
The **blade** is the sharp edge of a tool that cuts. A carving knife needs a very sharp **blade**.

blanket
A **blanket** is a large, soft cover. I snuggle under the **blankets** on a cold, winter night.

bleed
When you **bleed** you lose blood. When Jake fell down, his knee began to **bleed**. It **bled** all over his sock.

blow
1. When you **blow** you make the air move. Amy **blew** out the candles on her cake. "I'll huff and I'll puff and I'll **blow** your house down," said the wolf.
2. A **blow** is also a hard knock.

blue
Blue is the color of the sky on a clear, sunny day.

blunt
A knife that is not sharp is **blunt**. Cutting edges are **blunt** when they become worn down.

board
A **board** is a long, flat piece of wood. **Boards** are used to build things.

boat
The fishermen go to sea in a **boat**. **Boats** float on water.

This **boat** is made of **boards**.

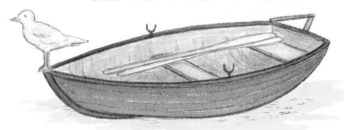

Big Bill has a strong **body** He is holding on to the ropes with **both** hands.

body
The whole of a person or animal is the **body**. Wrestlers have strong **bodies.**

boil
When water **boils** it becomes very hot. It bubbles and steams.

bomb
A **bomb** is a weapon that explodes. The **bomb** exploded and broke all the windows in the street.

bone
Our skeletons are made up of a framework of **bone**. There are 206 bones in your body.

book
Several sheets of paper can be folded into a **book.** I write in my class **books**. I read a **book** about a robot.

boomerang
A **boomerang** is a curved stick which the first people of Australia used for hunting. It comes back to the person who throws it.

boot
A **boot** is a strong, high shoe that protects your ankle and leg. Wear your **boots** to play in the snow.

borrow
Can I **borrow** your book? If I **borrow** it, I will keep it for a short time and then give it back.

both
The two of you can go shopping. You can **both** go shopping.

bottle
A **bottle** is usually made of glass. It holds liquids like juice and ketchup. "Pass me the **bottle** of soda, please."

bottom
The lowest part of something is the **bottom**. Jack fell down to the **bottom** of the hill.

Belinda loves to **bounce** on the trampoline. She is not afraid of hurting herself. She is **brave**.

bounce

If something can **bounce**, it can jump or spring back. Have you seen Jenny **bouncing** on the trampoline?

bow (rhymes with go)

1. Arrows are fired from a long, curved piece of wood called a **bow**.
2. Ribbons are tied in **bows. Bows** are made by looping the ribbon into a knot.
3. **Bow** (also rhymes with cow). When you bend over from the waist, you **bow**. The pianist **bowed** to the people and left the stage.

bowl

A **bowl** is a round, deep dish. We have a **bowl** of apples on the table.

box

A **box** is usually a cardboard or wooden container where objects can be stored. I have **boxes** filled with toys in my bedroom.

boy

A young male child is called a **boy**. When **boys** grow up they become men.

brain

Your **brain** is inside your head. You use your **brain** to think. The rest of your body sends messages to your **brain**.

branch

The **branch** of a tree spreads out from its trunk like arms. My rope ladder hangs from the **branches** of a tree.

brave

I am not afraid. I am feeling **brave**. It will be an act of **bravery**!

bread

Bread is eaten in many parts of the world. It is made from a mixture of flour and water. **Bread** is baked in an oven.

break

When something **breaks** it is smashed into pieces. I **broke** the plate. I didn't mean to **break** it. "Who's been sitting in my chair," cried Baby Bear, "and **broken** it into pieces?"

breakfast

The first meal of the day is called **breakfast.** We like to eat toast for **breakfast.**

Jack is a Scotsman. He eats porridge every morning for **breakfast.**

breath

Can you hold your **breath** for five seconds? Your **breath** is the air you push in and out of your lungs. When you do this you **breathe.**

brick

The walls of that house are made of **brick.** Clay is baked into **bricks** for building.

bridge

People cross a river on a **bridge.** Roads cross over other roads on **bridges.**

bright

Sunshine is very **bright.** It is full of light. The lamp is so **bright** it is hurting my eyes.

bring

To **bring** means to fetch or carry back. **Bring** some sausages home for the barbecue. Santa Claus **brought** everyone a present.

broom

A brush with a long handle is a **broom.** We sweep the floor with a **broom.** Witches are said to fly on **broomsticks.**

Brooms are for **brushing**, not flying!

My **brother** and I are boys, and we have the same mother and father.

brother

Although we have the same parents, my **brother** and I look very different.

brown

Brown is a color. Chocolate is a **brown** color and so is mud.

bruise

When I bumped my head a large **bruise** appeared. It was a large black-and-blue patch under the skin.

brush

A **brush** is a useful tool. In my house there are **toothbrushes**, **paintbrushes**, **hairbrushes**, scrubbing **brushes**, and **nailbrushes**. What would we do without **brushes**?

bubble

A **bubble** is a thin skin of liquid filled with gas. Fizzy drinks are full of **bubbles**.

bucket

You can carry lots of water in a **bucket**. **Buckets** are made of metal or plastic. We shall need a **bucket** of soapy water to clean the car. Pail is another word for **bucket**.

bug

A **bug** is an insect. Beetles are **bugs** that have hard folding wings. The wings fold over the body to make a tough cover.

build

Let's **build** a sandcastle. My uncle **built** this house. He put all the separate bits together to make a complete home. That **building** is very old. The **builder** died years ago.

Can you guess what all these different **brushes** are for?

35

bulb

1. A **bulb** is part of an electric lamp. Inside the glass **bulb** are the electric wires that light up.
2. **Bulbs** are also the round part of a plant that grows underground. Plant the **bulbs** in the spring.

bull

In the cattle family, the female is a cow and the male is a **bull**. A male elephant is also called a **bull**.
Beware of the **bull**; he is very bad-tempered.

bulldozer

The heap of earth was cleared away by the **bulldozer**. A **bulldozer** is a large tractor with special wheels and a big scoop in front.

A **bull** is looking at a **bulldozer**.

bullet

A small piece of metal which is shot from a gun is a **bullet**. The hunter carried spare **bullets** in his belt.

bump

You **bump** something when you knock against it. Jim is such a daydreamer that he **bumped** into the gatepost. We had a **bumpy** ride in the old car.

bunch

I gave my mom a **bunch** of flowers for her birthday. A **bunch** is a group of things joined together in some way. We bought three **bunches** of grapes.

bundle

A number of things tied together.

burn

Don't **burn** your fingers on the match! The fire will **burn** all night. Yesterday we **burned** some logs.

burst

The balloon **burst** with a loud bang. It broke open suddenly.

bury

To **bury** means to put something in a covered place. The children **buried** their dead mouse in the garden.

This big red **bus** is passing **by** Big Ben in London.

bus

Lots of passengers can be carried about in a **bus**. It is a large vehicle with rows of seats inside. London is famous for its red double-decker **buses.**

bush

A woody plant that is smaller than a tree is known as a **bush**. There are rose**bushes** in our garden.

busy

I have been **busy** all day helping Mom and Pop about the house. I have had a lot to do.

butter

The milk from the cows is whipped into **butter**. I spread **butter** on my toast.

butterfly

The **butterfly** is an insect with brightly colored wings. **Butterflies** fly in the daytime.

button

A **button** is a small, round thing. Shirts have **buttons** down the front. They are fixed into **buttonholes.**

buy

I will pay money for that hat and then it will be mine. I will **buy** it. I **bought** some gloves to keep my hands warm.

by

The table is **by** the bed. It is next to it. We traveled **by** train. The train will arrive **by** midnight.

We traveled **by** train, not **by** car.

Cc

cab

A **cab** is another word for a taxi. A **cab** is a car. You pay the driver to take you where you want to go.

cabbage

A **cabbage** is a vegetable with green leaves. Rabbits like to eat **cabbage**.

cactus

A **cactus** is a prickly plant that grows in the desert. Many **cacti** have brightly colored flowers.

A **cactus** and a **cabbage** are both plants.

We sat at the outdoor **café** and drank coffee.

café

We sat in the **café** and drank a cup of coffee. A **café** is a small restaurant. Sometimes the **café** has seats and tables on the sidewalk outside.

cage

A **cage** is an open box with metal or wooden bars. I don't like to see animals shut in **cages**.

cake

We eat **cake** for tea. Mother made the **cake** with flour, sugar and eggs. My favorite **cakes** are cup**cakes**.

calculator

A **calculator** is a counting machine that fits in your pocket. Can you divide a thousand by three on your **calculator**?

calendar

Look at the **calendar** and find out how many days there are in June. The **calendar** shows the days, weeks, and months of the year.

calf

A **calf** is a baby cow. A **calf** can also be a baby elephant, whale, or seal. The cow gave birth to two **calves.**

call

I will **call** his name and hope he hears. My name is Ben. What are you **called**?

camel

A **camel** is a large animal with one or two humps on its back. **Camels** are used to carry people and their goods through the desert.

A **camel's** hump is filled with fat. By using this fat a camel can go for a week without food or water.

camera

You use a **camera** to take photographs. I can take television pictures with my video **camera**.

camp

When a group of people live outdoors, they build a **camp**. The **camp**site was covered with tents. They set up **camp** by the river.

can

1. I **can** lift the dumbbells. I am able to lift them. I **can** climb that big tree. Please, may I climb it? Will you let me?
2. Many foods and drinks are stored in metal boxes called **cans**.

Canadian

A **Canadian** is a native or citizen of **Canada**. Canadians live in **Canada** or were born there.

canal

Boats and ships travel across the land on a **canal**. The **canal** was dug out like a long ditch and filled with water.

candy

Candy is a sweet food made from sugar and flavorings. Some **candies** are chocolate-covered. I like a **candy** bar for my snack.

canoe (ka-noo)

A **canoe** is a light, narrow boat. It is pointed at both ends. We paddled our **canoes** around the lake.

can't

Can't means cannot.

cap

1. The nurse wears a **cap** to keep her hair in place. A **cap** is a small hat. It is often worn by people who work in uniform.
2. You must remove the **cap** of a soda bottle before you can take a drink. A **cap** can also be a small lid.

capital

1. The **capital** city of France is Paris. The government of a country is in its **capital** city.
2. You can write the alphabet in **capital** letters. Anna starts with a **capital** A, but ant does not.

captain (kap-ten)

The leader of a group is usually called the **captain**. John is **captain** of the swimming team.

capture

To **capture** means to take prisoner. The hunters **captured** a wounded bear and took it to the zoo.

car

A **car** is a vehicle with an engine and four wheels. I can get four people in my **car**.

card

A **card** is a piece of stiff paper with some kind of writing or picture on it. We played Old Maid with a deck of playing **cards**. Send me a **postcard** from Spain.

cardboard

Cardboard is a stiffer paper than card. Boxes are made of **cardboard**.

carnival

Everyone enjoys a **carnival**. It is a festival with rides, games, and lots of good food.

At **carnivals** people dress up in colorful costumes.

carol

We sang a special Christmas song. We sang a **carol**. My favorite **carol** is "Away in a Manger."

carpenter

A person who works with wood making furniture or building houses, is a **carpenter**. We need a **carpenter** to fix the table.

Look at our dog's muddy pawmarks all over the **carpet**!

carpet

Don't let the muddy dog walk on the new **carpet**. The floor is covered with a large piece of cloth called a **carpet**.

carriage

A **carriage** was an old-fashioned vehicle that carried people. It was pulled by horses. A baby **carriage** stands on large wheels. The baby is pushed along the street in the **carriage**.

carry

Pick this box up and take it to the table. **Carry** it there. I **carried** the groceries out to the car.

cartoon

I always laugh at the "Peanuts" **cartoon**. I like those funny drawings of Charlie Brown and Snoopy. There are often Walt Disney **cartoons** on the television.

case

I packed a **case** to take on vacation. All my things were put in a leather box. My camera has its own **case** to protect it.

cash

Cash is the name given to paper money or coins. You use **cash** to buy things.

castle

A **castle** is a large building where people used to go for safety in time of war. Many kings and lords lived in **castles** in olden times.

Castles have thick stone walls

cat

Our pet **cat** likes to lie in the sun. A **cat** is a small, furry animal with a long tail. The **cat** family includes lions and other wild hunting **cats**.

catch

1. I can **catch** a ball in one hand. **Catch** means to get hold of something as it is moving. The police officer **caught** the robber.
2. You can also **catch** or get a cold.
3. To **catch** sometimes means to be on time for. I **caught** the bus to school.

caterpillar

A **caterpillar** looks like a furry worm. One day the **caterpillar** will change into a moth or a butterfly.

This is how a **caterpillar** changes into a beautiful butterfly.

A farmer driving **cattle**.

cattle

Cattle is the name given to a collection of cows. The farmer drove the **cattle** to the field.

cave

Sometimes there is a hole in a mountain or even underground. This is a **cave**. I like exploring **caves**.

ceiling

The inside of the roof of a room is the **ceiling**. We went to a church where the **ceiling** was painted with angels.

celebrate

Last week we had a party to **celebrate** my cousin's twenty-first birthday. Everyone likes to have a **celebration** to remember a special day.

cent

A **cent** is an American coin. One hundred **cents** make one dollar.

center

The middle of something is its **center**. The **center** of a city is always very crowded.

Most **centipedes** have between 15 and 23 pairs of legs.

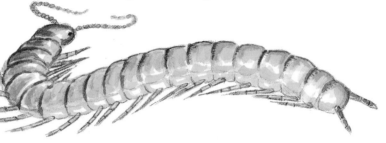

centipede

A **centipede** is a small wormlike creature that has lots of legs.

century

Another name for one hundred years is called a **century**.

cereal

We eat **cereal** for breakfast. This is food made from grains like wheat or oats.

certain

Certain means that you are sure of something. I am **certain** that all people have heads!

chain

A row of rings can be joined together to make a **chain**. A bicycle **chain** is made of metal. Sue wore a gold **chain**.

Our **cat** is sitting in the **center** of the **chair**.

chair

A **chair** is a piece of furniture we can sit on. Don't sit there – it's our cat's favorite **chair**.

champion

The winner is often called the **champion**. My sister is a **champion** swimmer.

change

To **change** means to make different. I wish you could **change** the weather. The frog **changed** into a handsome prince. I am **changing** into my sports clothes.

chase

Chase the rabbit out of the vegetable garden. You must run after it and try and catch it. Let's join in the **chase**.

43

chatter

1. Do not **chatter**! Stop talking on and on about things that are not at all important.
2. Sometimes your teeth rattle together when you are very cold. Your teeth are **chattering**.

cheap

When you buy something that is **cheap** it does not cost a lot of money. That jacket was expensive but this one was **cheap**.

check

When you **check**, you make sure that something is all right. Please **check** that the door is closed.

cheek

I drew a clown with a red **cheek** on each side of his face. **Cheeks** are the puffy parts of your face.

My picture of a clown has red **cheeks**.

cheerful

He's a **cheerful** person. He's always happy.

Cheese makes mice **cheerful**!

cheese

Cheese is a food made from milk. Some **cheeses** have mold in them and some have a strong smell.

cheetah

The **cheetah** is the fastest animal in the world. It is a member of the cat family. Its coat is covered with dark spots.

cherry

The fruit of the **cherry** tree is small and round. **Cherries** are picked when they are ripe.

chest

1. I puff out my **chest** when I take a deep breath. The **chest** is the top, front part of a person's body between the shoulders and the waist.
2. A **chest** is also a large, strong box. The pirates buried their treasure in a **chest**.

chicken
A **chicken** is a young hen.

child
Tom is the **child** of Mr. and Mrs. Brown. They have three young sons and daughters. There are three **children** in the family.

chimney
Smoke from the fire goes up through the **chimney**. **Chimneys** are tall funnels on a building through which smoke can escape.

Chimneys carry smoke away.

chimpanzee
A **chimpanzee** is a kind of ape. **Chimpanzees** live in Africa.

chin
Your **chin** is the part of the face that sticks out below your mouth. Pop's **chin** is covered by a beard.

china
China is the kind of earth from which cups and saucers are made. Let's use the **china** coffee cups.

chocolate
Chocolate is made from the beans of the cacao tree. The beans are crushed into **chocolate** powder. A **chocolate** bar is my favorite snack.

choose
Choose means to pick out one thing from many others. Sam **chose** the blue pencil.

Christmas
At **Christmas** people called Christians celebrate the birth of Jesus Christ.

Children in **church** at **Christmas**.

church
Some people go to **church** each Sunday. Christian people worship in **churches**.

All the fun of the **circus** with acrobats, clowns, and elephants.

circle

A **circle** is a round shape. The dancers all skipped in a **circle**.

circus

The **circus** is coming to town. It is a traveling show with clowns and acrobats. The **circus** is held in a large tent.

city

A very large town is called a **city**. The capital **city** of Italy is Rome. **Cities** have big office blocks.

clap

Clap your hands together in time with the music. Beat your hands together. Everyone **clapped** at the end of the show.

classroom

My class meets in the **classroom** for its lessons. The rooms in a school are called **classrooms**.

claw

This cat has its **claw** caught in my sweater. Some animals have pointed nails on their feet called **claws**.

clean

I have removed all the dirt from the floor. I have **cleaned** it. A **clean** floor is not dirty.

clear

I can see what is inside this bottle because the glass is **clear**. The glass is easy to see through.

clever

What a bright, intelligent child! This child is really **clever**.

cliff

A high, rocky **cliff** rose above the sea. A **cliff** is a high, steep rockface where the land meets the sea.

climb

The students learned to **climb** a steep cliff. They learned how to go up it using their hands and feet to hold on. The girls **climbed** the ropes.

clock

Look at the **clock** and see what time it is. It is 3 o'clock. A machine that tells the time is called a **clock**.

close

1. To **close** means to shut. The teacher **closed** the door. A door that is **closed** is not open.

2. Close can also mean near. My house is **close** to the park.

closet

The guest left her coat in the **closet. Closets** are small rooms for coats.

cloth

Cloth is something that is made of wool or cotton. Clothes are made of **cloth**.

clothes

My suitcase is full of summer **clothes.** It is full of things to wear.

cloud

There is a big white **cloud** in the sky. A **cloud** is made of tiny water drops. Dark **clouds** often bring heavy rain and thunderstorms.

clown

A **clown** is a funny person at the circus who makes you laugh. The **clowns** emptied buckets of water over each other.

What time does the **clown's clock** show?
The other **clown** is throwing rings that are shaped like **circles**.

My friend and I belong to a model airplane **club**.

club

A group of people meet at a **club** to enjoy their special interest. All my friends belong to the model airplane **club**.

clumsy

A **clumsy** person often knocks things down or bumps against things. That **clumsy** donkey has kicked over his food bucket.

coach

Our **coach** is teaching us how to dive from the top board. A **coach** is a trainer or teacher.

coal

Coal is a special kind of black rock. It is dug from the ground and burned to make heat.

coast

The place where the land meets the sea is called the **coast**. The ship sailed around the **coast** of Norway.

coat

A **coat** is a piece of clothing you wear outdoors. Put your arms in each sleeve and do up the buttons.

cobweb

A spider spins a fine net to catch insects for its dinner. It spins a **cobweb**.

This **cobweb** was spun by a spider.

coconut

The hard, brown nut of the **coconut** palm is called a **coconut**. You can crack the **coconut** shell and eat the soft white fruit inside.

coffee

The beans of the **coffee** plant are picked and roasted. **Coffee** beans are crushed into a powder which we mix with hot water and drink.

This king **collects coins**.

coin

A metal piece of money is called a **coin**. This **coin** is worth twenty-five cents. Four of these **coins** equal one dollar.

cold

1. On a **cold** day the weather is not warm. You must keep the ice cream **cold** or it will melt.
2. If you have a **cold**, you sneeze and feel unwell.

collar

My dog wears a **collar**. It is the band that goes around its neck. Your shirt has a red collar.

collect

When you bring things together you **collect** them. I am **collecting** stamps from all over the world. Have you seen his **collection** of foreign coins?

color

Red, blue, green, and yellow are all **colors**. Which is your favorite **color**?

comb

A **comb** is a small object with "teeth" that is used to straighten out hair. I **combed** my dog and it looks very good.

The **colors** of the rainbow are: red, orange, yellow, green, blue, indigo and violet.

come

To **come** means to move toward or to reach. My dog will **come** when I call it. John **came** to our house to see our new puppy. Are you **coming** to the party? What a lot of **coming** and going in the street.

comfortable

My bed is so **comfortable**. It is warm and soft. I feel good in it.

comic

I buy a **comic** book each week. It has pages of funny stories and drawings inside. Things that are **comic** make us laugh.

I read my **comic** book. A **comic** book tells stories with pictures.

compass

An instrument that is used for finding the way is called a **compass**. The needle on a **compass** always points to the north.

computer

A **computer** does calculations and stores information. All the information about train times is stored in the **computer**.

concert

A **concert** is a musical show. The band gave a **concert** in the park.

Connie the **conjurer** is pulling rabbits out of her hat.

conjurer

A **conjurer** performs tricks that look like magic. The **conjurer** pulled a rabbit out of a hat.

cook

Cook means to make food ready to eat. Food is hot when it is **cooked**.

cookie

A **cookie** is a flat, sweet-tasting cake. I like raisin cookies best.

The goose on the right is a **copy** of the goose on the left. They are exactly the same.

copy

A **copy** looks exactly like something else. Please make a **copy** of this map so that we both know the way. Would you like two **copies** instead?

corner

Two straight lines meet at a **corner**. Turn the **corner** and you'll be on the main street. There is a fly sitting in the **corner** of this page.

correct

An answer is **correct** when it is right. It has no mistakes in it.

cost

The **cost** is how much you pay for something. What does this hat **cost**?

This fly is sitting in the **corner** of this page.

My brother Nick wears a monster **costume**.

My ghost **costume** is made from a **cotton** sheet.

costume

When you dress up in special clothes for a special occasion, you put on a **costume**. Nick went to the party in a monster **costume**.

cotton

The fluffy part of the **cotton** seed is woven into material. I wear **cotton** dresses in summer.

cough (coff)

A **cough** is a noise you make when air suddenly rushes from your chest.

I can't **count** the stars. Clouds are **covering** them.

count

To **count** means to add up. Can you **count** the number of stars in the sky? How many stars are there?

country

1. We each live in an area of land called a **country**. My **country** is Spain, so I am Spanish.
2. The land outside the cities and towns is called the **country**. There are fields and trees in the **country**.

couple

A **couple** means two of the same thing. It means the same as a pair. I have a **couple** of tame lizards.

cousin

My **cousin** is the child of my uncle and aunt. John and his **cousin** went to see their grandma.

cover

If you **cover** something you put something over it to hide or protect it. The sky was **covered** by clouds.

cow

A **cow** is the female member of the cattle family. A **cow** can also be a female whale, moose, or elephant. **Cows** give us milk to drink.

cowboy

The **cowboy** rode out to count the herd. The men who take care of herds of cattle are called **cowboys**.

crab

A **crab** is a sea creature with a shell. It has a flat body and sharp claws. It's not easy to catch a **crab**!

crack

A narrow opening is called a **crack**. There is a **crack** in this saucer. We entered the cave through a **crack** in the rocks.

The **crab** is **crawling** toward my baby sister.

cracker

I ate a **cracker** and cheese for my snack. A **cracker** is a thin, crisp wafer or biscuit.

My baby sister is **crawling** toward the **crab**.

The **cowboys** are rounding up the cattle to take them to market.

crane

A **crane** is a tall machine that can lift very heavy objects. It has a long arm that can move up and down.

crash

When things bang into each other, they **crash**. The ball hit the window with a **crash**.

crawl

My baby sister can **crawl** but she cannot walk yet. She moves forwards very slowly on her hands and knees.

cream

1. Joe likes whipped **cream** on his pie. **Cream** is the rich, fatty part of the milk.
2. Dad puts **cream** on his face when he shaves. Special **creams** make the skin soft.

creature

A person or animal is known as a living **creature**. There are lots of tiny **creatures** living under this stone.

crocodile

A **crocodile** has a long body that is covered with scales. Its jaw is filled with sharp teeth. It has short legs. **Crocodiles** live in water.

crooked

Things that are bent are often **crooked**. That line isn't straight – it's **crooked**.

cross

1. If one line passes over another, it makes a **cross**. The teacher put a **cross** by every wrong sum. We **crossed** the road when the traffic warden told us to.
2. Jim was rude to his brother and made him **cross**. When you feel **cross** you are angry.

crowd

A large number of people all together is called a **crowd**. A **crowd** gathered to see the movie star.

cruel

People who give pain to others are **cruel**. The man was **cruel** when he hit his horse.

crumb

You can break bread and cakes into tiny pieces. Each piece is called a **crumb**. We give **crumbs** to the birds in winter.

crush

If you **crush** something, you press on it hard and break it into pieces. Jim crushed slices of bread to make **crumbs**.

cry

1. When tears come from your eyes, you **cry**. I **cried** when I hurt my ankle.
2. Did you hear the girl **cry** for help? When you call or shout, you **cry** out.

crystal

A **crystal** is the shape which tiny pieces of many things take. Salt and sugar **crystals** have different shapes.

cube

Dice are shaped like **cubes**. A **cube** is a solid thing with six sides all the same size.

cup

We drink coffee from a **cup**. A **cup** is a small bowl with a handle. Sometimes silver **cups** are given as prizes.

cure

Cure means to make well. The hot lemon drink **cured** my cold.

curl

A twisted ring shape is called a **curl**. My sister **curls** her hair. My dog's coat is long and **curly**.

It is the **custom** for American Indians to carry their babies on their backs.

curve

When a line bends round in one direction, it makes a **curve**. The river **curved** around the hill.

cushion

You will be more comfortable if you sit on a **cushion**. A **cushion** is a cloth bag filled with soft material.

custom

A **custom** is the usual way of doing something. In China it is the **custom** to eat food with chopsticks. It was the **custom** for American Indians to carry their babies or papooses on their backs.

cut

When you divide something with a sharp blade, you **cut** it. **Cut** me a slice of cake. The doctor **cut** open the bandage. Uncle Jack is **cutting** his fingernails.

cycle

I like to ride on my bicycle. I like to **cycle**.

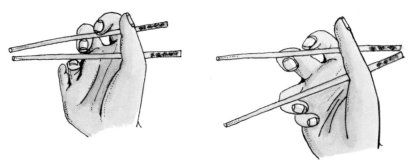

It is the **custom** in China to eat with chopsticks.

Dd

daffodil

A **daffodil** is a tall yellow flower. **Daffodils** grow in springtime.

dagger

A **dagger** is a sharp knife. It was used for fighting in olden times. The Roman gladiator pulled out his **dagger** to attack the lion.

dam

A large wall which is built to block a flow of water is called a **dam**. The **dam** stopped the flood waters from rushing down the valley. The beavers built a **dam** of twigs and weed across the stream.

Beavers build **dams** across streams.

damp

Something that feels wet is said to be **damp**. John came in from the rain and hung up his **damp** coat to dry.

dangerous

Things that are **dangerous** can harm you. To skate on thin ice is very **dangerous**.

dark

As the sun goes down, the sky becomes **dark**. **Dark** things are without light. He has **dark** hair.

dart

1. Dan threw his **darts** on the board to score twenty points. **Darts** are small pointed arrows.
2. To **dart** also means to move suddenly and quickly. Sue **darted** into the bushes and hid.

date

1. A **date** is the sticky fruit of the **date** palm. I ate a whole box of **dates**.

2. The **date** of Dan's birthday is March 24. The **date** tells you the day, the month, and the year when something happens.

daughter (daw-ter)

A **daughter** is a female child. I would like your **daughter** to meet my son.

day

1. Each **day** starts at midnight and lasts until the next midnight. There are twenty-four hours in each **day**. There are seven **days** in each week. Each **day** has a special name.

2. **Day** is also the time when it is light outside, between sunrise and sunset.

dead

An animal or plant that is not alive is **dead**. I rescued the bird from our cat before it was **dead**. The **death** of the bird made us all unhappy.

deaf

A person who is **deaf** cannot hear. I talked to the **deaf** man, using my fingers and hands to make signs.

December

December is the twelfth and last month of the year.

The **date** of Christmas Day is December 25.

On which **day** of the week are New Year's Day and Thanksgiving Day?

decide

If you make up your mind to do something you **decide** to do it. Nick **decided** to buy a dictionary.

deck

1. The part of a ship where you walk is called the **deck**. The diver jumped off the **deck**
2. **Deck** also means a set of playing cards.

The diver jumped off the ship's **deck** into the **deep** sea.

deep

The water went down very far. It was **deep**. There was a **deep** valley between the mountains.

deer

A **deer** is an animal that lives in the woods. Male red **deer** grow strong antlers on their heads.

delicious

The raspberry pie was **delicious**. It tasted good.

den

A **den** is a hideout for a wild animal. The bear passed the winter in its **den**.

dentist

The **dentist** looks after your teeth. I went to the **dentist** to have a tooth filled.

desert

A **desert** is a large area of land where there is little rain or water. It is so dry in the **desert** that few trees and plants can grow there. Many **deserts** are very hot and covered with sand.

desk

A **desk** is a worktable with drawers. Ben keeps his secret diary in the top drawer of his **desk**.

I keep my **dictionary** in my **desk**.

A **detective** at work.

detective

The **detective** found the missing necklace. **Detectives** try to work out who did a robbery or murder.

diamond

A **diamond** costs a lot of money. It is a kind of stone. Most diamonds have no color, but they sparkle in the light. **Diamonds** are often used in jewelry.

dice

To play many board games you need a pair of **dice**. Each **die** is a cube whose sides are covered with different numbers of dots. You must throw the **dice** to start the game.

dictionary

This book filled with words and their meanings is called a **dictionary**. **Dictionaries** tell you how to spell words.

did See **do**.

die

We took our sick dog to the vet, since we didn't want it to **die**. When a living thing **dies**, it stops living. I think that plant is **dying**. Has it already **died**?

different

Something that is **different** is not the same. I would rather have a jacket that is **different** from my brother's. When Mom goes to the hairdresser, she comes home looking **different**.

difficult

A **difficult** question is not easy to answer. Carol tried to knit some socks but the pattern was too **difficult**.

Dice are cubes. They are marked on each side with from one to six dots.

Katherine is **digging** in the garden. Be careful! Don't get dirty!

dig

If you were to **dig** deep enough, you would **dig** through to the other side of the world. I don't believe anyone has ever **dug** that far. Perhaps someone is still **digging**!

dinner

Dinner is one of the meals we eat each day. Sometimes we eat in a **dining** room.

dinosaur

You will never see a live **dinosaur**. **Dinosaurs** were large animals that lived on land a long, long time ago.

dirty

Dirty things are not clean. Your clothes are covered with **dirt**.

disappear

To **disappear** means to vanish. The conjurer said the magic word and the rabbit **disappeared**. We could not see it anymore.

discover

I want to **discover** something about the stars. I want to find out something new. Christopher Columbus made a great **discovery**!

discuss

I want to talk to you about my plans. I want to **discuss** them with you. The two men had a long **discussion** about old times.

A huge **dinosaur**. It has a very large body and a very small head. Have you ever seen a **dinosaur**?

disguise

When you **disguise** yourself you try to change how you look. The robber **disguised** himself as the bank manager.

dish

A **dish** is a plate. The **dishes** were piled with apples.

distance

The **distance** between two places is the length between them. The **distance** between my house and yours is half a mile.

disturb

I was fast asleep until the cat **disturbed** me. When you **disturb** someone you stop them from doing what they are doing. People get annoyed when they are **disturbed**.

ditch

The farmer dug a **ditch** to drain the water off the field. A **ditch** is a narrow channel that usually holds water.

dive

To **dive** means to jump into water head first. He **dived** into the pool from the top board.

divide

To **divide** means to share and split into smaller parts. Mike **divided** the toffee bar into four pieces. I have to **divide** 493 by 9. What a difficult **division** problem!

do

When you **do** something you carry out an action. Are you going to **do** your homework? Yes, I am **doing** it now. I **did** send the letter even if you think I **didn't**. The mice have **done** a lot of damage to the cheese.

doctor

When Jane was sick she went to see the **doctor**. A **doctor** is somebody who cures sick people.

dog

A **dog** is a hairy animal. Wolves, jackals and foxes are relations of **dogs**. My **dog** barks when it is happy.

My **dog** has found a hole in the ground. It wants to know what is inside.

doll

Children have played with **dolls** for hundreds of years. A **doll** is a toy model of a person.

These **dolls** are sitting down.

dollar

The **dollar** is the name of the money used in the United States. In Canada, Australia, and New Zealand money is also called **dollars**.

done See **do**

donkey

A **donkey** is an animal closely related to the horse. **Donkeys** have long ears and make a loud braying noise that sounds like ee-aw.

door

A **door** opens and closes the entrance in something. **Doors** are often made of wood or glass. She stood in the **doorway** and asked if she could come in. There is a mat on the **doorstep** to wipe your shoes.

dot

A **dot** is a tiny point. I watched him drive away until the car was no bigger than a **dot.**

double

1. John asked for a **double** helping. He asked for twice as much.
2. Have you ever met your **double**? Your **double** is someone who looks exactly like you.

doughnut (doe-nut)

A **doughnut** is a fat, round cake which is fried in fat then covered in sugar.

down

When you go **down** you go to a lower place. "Jack and Jill fell **down** the hill." **Down** is the opposite of up.

This soldier is going **downstairs**.

downstairs

We climb stairs between the floors of a building. We go **downstairs** to a lower floor. **Downstairs** is the opposite of upstairs.

dozen

Another name for 12 is a **dozen**.

drag

The log was so heavy we had to **drag** it along with a tractor. To **drag** means to pull roughly along the ground.

dragon

A **dragon** is a make-believe animal that appears in lots of old stories. **Dragons** were said to be large, scaly creatures that breathed fire through their noses.

drain

A **drain** is a pipe that takes dirty water away. Pour the bucket of dirty water down the **drain**.

Can you **draw** a picture of a **dragon**?

drank See drink

draw

I **draw** pictures on pieces of paper, using my pencil and crayons. I **drew** a picture of my brother. Would you like to see my **drawing**?

drawer

A **drawer** is a box in which things are kept. A chest has **drawers** which you can pull out or push in.

I **dreamed** I was a piece of cheese!

dream

Sometimes, while you are asleep, you think of all kinds of things. These imaginings are **dreams**. In my **dream** I flew to the moon on an elephant. I **dreamed** I was a piece of cheese. John didn't hear the question as he was too busy **day-dreaming**.

dress

1. A **dress** is a piece of clothing worn by girls and women. Jane and Carol both wore blue **dresses** to the party.
2. To **dress** means to put on clothes. Jim got **dressed** before breakfast.

drill

A **drill** is a machine for making holes. The carpenter **drilled** four holes in the wood.

drink

When you swallow liquid, you **drink**. **Drink** the medicine and you'll feel better. Jeff **drank** it all up. When he had **drunk** it, he felt better. Who's been **drinking** my orange juice?

drip

Water **drips** when it falls in spots. The rain is **dripping** onto the floor. Drops of water **dripped** off the umbrella.

drive

Can you **drive** a car? Can you steer it along the road? The **driver drove** us to the beach. I have been **driving** for six hours. The car was being **driven** too fast.

drop

Drop means to let something fall. Luke **dropped** a glass on the floor.

drown

People **drown** by breathing in water instead of air. Their lungs become filled with water and they die. The boy **drowned** when he fell into the pool.

drum

A **drum** is a musical instrument that makes a loud bang when it is hit. **Drums** are made from skins stretched over hollow boxes.

dry

Something that is **dry** holds no **water**. **Dry** things are not wet. The hairdresser **dried** my hair. The clean clothes are **drying** on the line.

duck

A **duck** is a bird that lives near water. The **ducks** were swimming on the pond. **Ducks** have specially shaped feet which help them to swim.

dull

Things are **dull** when they are gray or uninteresting. What a **dull** day. It is raining and there is nothing to do.

during

1. The play was so dull, I slept **during** the whole first act. **During** means throughout.
2. **During** the second act, a conjurer did a trick. **During** can also mean at some time in.

dust

Tiny pieces of dirt that move round easily when they are blown are called **dust**. I must clean the table with a **duster**. It is covered with **dust**.

dwarf

A **dwarf** is a tiny person, animal, or plant. **Dwarfs** do not grow to full size. Jane planted a **dwarf** tree in the window box.

Can you see the **dwarf** fishing in the **duck-pond**?

Ee

each

Each of us bought a ticket for the game. **Each** means every person.

eagle

The **eagle** is a large bird of prey. The bald **eagle** is the national sign of the United States of America.

ear

You have an **ear** on each side of your head. You hear things with your **ears**.

early

The visitors arrived **early**. They arrived in good time. The birds wake **early** in the morning. **Early** also means at the beginning of the day.

earring

You wear **earrings** on your ears. My sister wore long golden **earrings**.

Earrings

earth

1. We live on one of the planets that move around the sun. Our planet is called **earth**.
2. The gardener planted new seeds in the **earth**. Seeds are planted in the soil, which is another word for **earth**.

east

East is where the sun rises in the morning. **East** is one of the four directions on a compass: north, south, **east**, and west.

Easter

Christian people celebrate **Easter** in memory of the day Jesus Christ rose from the dead. **Easter** comes on a Sunday in March or April. At **Easter** we all received **Easter** eggs.

easy

Things that are simple to do are **easy**. This math problem is not at all difficult. It is very **easy**.

All living creatures must **eat**.

eat

We **eat** food when we are hungry. We put the food in our mouth and chew it and swallow it. The rabbit **ate** a carrot. Have you **eaten** your spinach? I am **eating** the bread and leaving the hard crust.

echo

An **echo** is made when a sound bounces off high walls. I shouted in the cave and the sound **echoed** back again and again.

edge

The part along the end or side of something is the **edge**. I walked along the **edge** of the cliff. To sew around the cushion stitch the **edges** together.

egg

Birds lay **eggs**. Eggs are made of shell. An **egg** holds a baby bird until it is born.

The **eggs** in this nest cannot fall over the **edge**.

eight (8)

Eight is a number. Four and four equals eight. August is the **eighth** month of the year. Spiders have **eight** legs.

either

When you choose between two things, you choose **either** one thing or the other. You may have **either** an apple or a pear.

Will **either** of you two children take me for a walk, please?

elastic

A belt made of **elastic** will stretch. **Elastic** things stretch to a bigger size then return to normal. **Elastic** is usually made of rubber.

elbow

Your **elbow** is the bony part of the arm between the upper and lower bones. It is where your arm bends.

electricity

Electricity is a form of power that moves along wires. All kinds of machines in the home are made to work by **electricity**. Do you use an **electric** toothbrush?

elephant

The **elephant** is the largest animal on earth. Its tusks are used for digging and fighting. Its trunk holds things very tightly.

elevator

An **elevator** is a machine. It lifts people from floor to floor in a tall building.

An **elf** is sitting on the **end** of an **enormous elephant's** trunk.

elf

An **elf** is a small, magical character who appears in storybooks. **Elves** are usually very naughty.

empty

The bag is **empty**. There is nothing in it. The opposite of **empty** is full.

end

The **end** comes at the finish. At the **end** of the play, the people clapped. Take the **end** of the rope and pull! The story had a happy **ending**.

enemy

The French went to war against the **enemy**. People who fight you are called the **enemy**. I hope you have no **enemies**.

engine

A machine that makes power to pull and push is called an **engine**. The racing car had a powerful **engine**. The **engine** was repaired at the garage.

enjoy

Don gets a lot of pleasure from playing the trumpet. He **enjoys** playing in the band. I **enjoyed** the party. You **enjoy** all your hobbies.

enormous

Something that is **enormous** is very, very big. The ant thought the elephant was **enormous**.

enough

James did not want any more pie, as he had eaten **enough**. If you have **enough** you have as much as you need.

enter

To **enter** means to come in. We are **entering** the fairground. The actress **entered** to loud cheers.

envelope

A letter is mailed in an **envelope**. An **envelope** is a paper covering for a letter. I wrote the address on the **envelope**.

equal

Things that are **equal** are the same as each other. Six is **equal** to half a dozen.

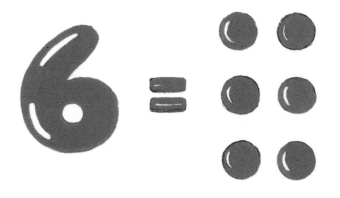

Two lines like this make the sign for **equals**. The number 6 is an **even** number.

erupt

When something explodes violently it **erupts**. The volcano **erupted** and covered the countryside with ash.

escalator

An **escalator** is a moving staircase. Make sure you hold the rail while riding on the **escalator**!

escape

The prisoner tried to **escape** from the prison. To **escape** means to get free or get away from something.

Eskimos are people who live in cold Arctic lands. They wear fur clothes to keep warm.

Eskimo

Some people who live in the Arctic Circle are known as **Eskimos**. They cut blocks of ice to make a house. It is called an igloo.

even

1. **Even** numbers, like 2, 4, and 6, can be divided equally by 2. The other numbers are called odd numbers.
2. **Even** can also mean equal. The score was **even** at the end of the game.

evening

The part of the day when the sun sets is called **evening**. He left home during the **evening**.

event

When something important happens it is an **event**. When people invented the wheel, it was a great **event** in history.

The **evil** witch hates **everybody** and **everything**.

ever

Snow White and the Prince lived happily **ever** after. They were always happy. **Ever** can also mean at any time. Have you **ever** seen a ghost?

every

Every means each one. **Every** year that passes makes you one year older.

everybody

Everybody has a birthday once a year. All people have a birthday. **Everybody** gets older as time passes, nobody gets younger.

everything

Everything in the basket was for Red Riding Hood's grandma. All the things means the same as **everything**.

everywhere

To search **everywhere** means to search in every place. When the river flooded, there was water **everywhere**.

evil

Evil people are very, very bad. The **evil** fairy cast a bad spell on Sleeping Beauty.

excellent

She got **excellent** marks in her history test. **Excellent** means very good. This is an **excellent** picture of the man.

excited

When you feel **excited** you feel happy. Joe was so **excited** he clapped his hands with joy.

Joe is **excited**. He has a present.

71

excuse

If you don't want to do something, you must find a reason, or an **excuse**, for not doing it. What is your **excuse** for being late at school?

Every morning Matt does his keep-fit **exercises**.

exercise

An activity that helps you learn or keep fit is called an **exercise**. She does keep-fit **exercises** to lose weight. My dog gets **exercise** in the park. These piano **exercises** are easy.

exit

The way out is the **exit**. Take the door marked "**Exit**" to get out of the hall.

expect

When you think that the train will come you **expect** it to arrive. You **expect** things that you think will happen. She **expected** to get a new bicycle for Christmas.

expensive

Things that cost a lot of money to buy are **expensive**. I would like that train, but it's too **expensive**.

explain

The teacher will **explain** how electricity makes a light bulb glow. She will make it clear to us how this happens.

explode

When a bomb **explodes**, it blows up. Things that **explode** break into pieces with a loud noise. This is called an **explosion**.

This woman is an **explorer**. She is looking for new kinds of plants in the forest.

explore

Explore means to look carefully around a place where you have not been before. Jane and John **explored** the garden of their new house.

extra

I would like more cheese. I would like an **extra** piece.

I would like another cherry. I would like an **extra** one.

I have blue **eyes**. My **eyelids** cover my **eyeballs**. There are **eyelashes** at the end of my **eyelids**. The hair that grows above my eye is called my **eyebrow**.

Thread goes through the **eye** of a needle.

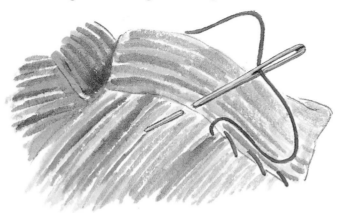

eye

I have one right **eye** and one left **eye**. My **eyesight** is how I see. The hair growing over my **eye** is an **eyebrow**. A fringe of hairs called **eyelashes** also protect the eye. The **eyelids** close over the **eye** when you blink or go to sleep.

73

Ff

face

Your **face** is the front part of your head. Do you know all the parts of your **face**? Eyes, mouth, nose, chin, cheek, forehead. To see your **face** you look in a mirror.

fact

A **fact** is something that really happens. It is a **fact** that George Washington was the first President of the United States.

factory

A **factory** is a place where people work together to make things. Bicycles are made in **factories.**

fair

1. She has **fair** hair. It is a light color.
2. **Fair** can also mean to act in a way that seems to be right. The judge made a **fair** decision and let the prisoner free.

My eyes, nose, and mouth are parts of my **face**. My hair is **fair**.

fairy

A **fairy** can do magic things. **Fairies** are tiny, magical creatures that appear in old stories.

fall

1. Be careful you don't **fall** off the wall! When something **falls**, it drops.
2. The **fall** is another name for autumn. It comes between summer and winter.

false

False means the same as not true or not real. He is wearing a **false** beard.

family

Your **family** includes your mother and father, your sisters and brothers and all the people who are related to you.

famous

Famous people are well-known. After Jim appeared on television, he became **famous**.

far

A place that is a long way off is **far**. The pirates searched **far** and wide to find the hidden treasure.

farm

On a **farm**, crops are grown and animals are looked after. The person in charge of the **farm** is the **farmer**.

Things to eat come from **farms**.

fast

When something moves quickly, it moves **fast**. Mary ran **faster** than Joe and won the race.

fat

Fat people are big all around. That **fat** man won't fit in the chair. If you eat too much, you will get **fat**. **Fat** is the opposite of thin.

father

A **father** is a male parent. Your **father** and mother are your parents. **Fathers** are often called "Dad" by their children.

fault

I broke the cup. It is my **fault** that it is broken.

favorite

Your **favorite** things are those you like best. What is your **favorite** color?

Fred says he has become too **fat**. He is going to stop eating so much.

Wing **feathers** help birds to fly.

feather

A bird has **feathers** all over its body. Its wings are made of long **feathers**. This pillow is filled with **feathers**.

February

The second month of the year is **February**. St. Valentine's Day is on **February** 14, when people send each other loving messages.

feed

To **feed** means to give food to. Have you **fed** the cat today?

feel

1. When you touch things, you **feel** them. Laura **felt** the cold snowball. This table **feels** very smooth.
2. Things that happen make us **feel** happy or sad. John **felt** happy when he went to see a football game. You would not speak to me. You hurt my **feelings**.

feet

Feet means more than one foot. Dogs have four **feet**.

female

A **female** is a girl or a woman. Animals are either male or **female**.

fence

A **fence** is a barrier. There is often a **fence** around a garden. We climbed the **fence** to reach the apple tree.

fetch

We told the dog to go and get the stick and bring it back to us. We told him to **fetch** it.

few

When there are only a **few**, there are not very many. There are only a **few** kinds of animals that can live in the desert.

field

A **field** is a large area where grass or crops grow. Cows are kept in the **fields**.

There are only a **few** cows in the field. There are only three.

This bull is **fierce**.

fierce

The bull looked very angry and frightening. It was **fierce**.

fight

The boys began to quarrel and **fight**. When people **fight**, they attack each other angrily. I am sorry I **fought** with my sister yesterday.

figure

A **figure** is a sign for a number like the **figures** 2 and 5.

fill

Fill the basket with potatoes. To **fill** means to take up all the space inside something. The crowds **filled** the building. The arena was **full**.

film

A **film** is another word for a movie. **Film** is also the roll of plastic material used to take photographs.

fin

A bony **fin** sticks out of the top and sides of a fish's body. Fish use their **fins** to help them steer underwater.

find

When you come across something that was lost, you **find** it. Can you **find** Jupiter in the night sky? He **found** the way across the mountains without a map.

fine

On a **fine** day it is sunny and warm. **Fine** means very good or excellent.

finger

I am wearing a ring on my **finger**. Human beings have five **fingers** at the end of each hand.

You have five **fingers** at the end of each hand. You can also say you have four **fingers** and one thumb. Which is your thumb?

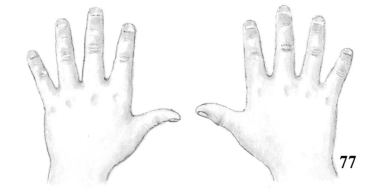

finish

To **finish** means to come to the end. When you **finish** the jigsaw, you will have put every piece in place. Mary **finished** her homework.

fir

A **fir** is a kind of tree that never loses all its leaves. Forests of **fir** trees grow in northern countries of the world.

fire

A **fire** is made when things burn. Let's burn all the wood on a **fireplace.**

When **fires** burn they make **flames,** and give off heat and light.

fire engine

The truck that races to a fire carrying the pumps and ladders is called a **fire engine.**
Firefighters travel to the fire on the **fire engines.**

first

First, we set out the cups, then we made tea. **First** means the same as at the beginning. January is the **first** month of the year.

fish

A **fish** is an animal that lives in water. **Fish** are cold-blooded and they breathe through flaps on the body called gills.

fist

When you close your hand tightly into a ball it forms a **fist.** The fighters hit each other with their **fists.**

fit

1. To be **fit** is to be well and healthy. Get plenty of exercise to keep **fit.**
2. To **fit** also means to be the right size or shape. This coat **fits** me very well.

My Mom's coat is too big for me. It does not **fit** me at all!

five (5)

Five is a number. You have five fingers on each hand.

flashlight

A flashlight is a lamp that needs batteries to work. It is small enough to carry around.

Five flags flapping in the wind.

flag

A flag is a sign made of cloth. Each country has its own flag. At the Olympic Games, the flags of many countries fly over the arena.

flake

A flake is a small, light piece of something. Snowflakes fell all over the grass.

flame

A flame is made when gas burns. Bright orange flames rose from the fire.

flap

1. A flap is a cover or lid which moves over an opening. There is a flap over the letterbox to stop the rain getting in.
2. To flap also means to beat. The bird flapped its wings and flew into the sky.

flat

A flat surface has no bumps. The countryside was so flat, the walkers could see for miles. A flat tire has no air left in it.

flavor

The flavor of food is the way it tastes. I chose four different flavors of ice cream.

float

To float means to be held up in the air or on the surface of water. A boat floats on the sea. The balloon is floating in the air.

Birds flap their wings to fly.

79

floor

The **floor** of a room is the part you walk on. In my bedroom, I have a red rug on the **floor**. Jack's room is on the third **floor**.

flour

The seeds of wheat and other grains are crushed into a powder called **flour**. We use **flour** to make bread and cakes.

flower

A **flower** is formed from the colorful petals of a plant. **Flowers** attract insects to the plant.

Many **flowers** have a lovely smell.

fly

1. Birds **fly** through the air. They move in the air using their wings. A jet plane **flew** over the city. It is **flying** high up above the clouds.
2. A **fly** is an insect. Cover up the food, so the **flies** cannot get to it.

A **foal** with its mother.

foal

A **foal** is a baby horse. The **foal** stayed close to its mother until it had learned to run.

fog

Fog forms when many drops of water hang in the air in a thick mist. It is difficult to see ahead when it is foggy.

fold

When you bend one part of something over another part you **fold** it. Tim **folded** the paper in half.

follow

To **follow** means to go behind. My dog **follows** me everywhere.

food

We eat **food** to stay alive. I like some kinds of **food** more than others.

foot

Your **foot** is the part of your body which you place on the ground when you walk. You have two **feet**.

football

Football is a game played by two teams on a large field. It is played with a ball called a **football**.

footprint

When we step on soft ground, we leave a mark called a **footprint.** The farmer found the fox's **footprints** near the henhouse.

Footprints made by my **feet** in the sand.

forehead (for-red)

The part of your face above your eyes is your **forehead**.

forest

An area where many trees grow close together is called a **forest**. We followed the path through the **forest**.

forget

Those things you cannot remember are the ones you **forget**. I keep **forgetting** how old I am.
I **forgot** to go to the dentist today.
I have **forgotten** how to tie a bow.

fork

A **fork** is a tool for picking up food. A **fork** has points or prongs which spear the food.

fortune

1. A **fortune** usually describes a large amount of money.
2. Your **fortune** can also describe what will happen to you.

forward

When you go **forward** you move ahead and to the front. **Forward** is the opposite of backward.

fountain

A **fountain** is a spray of water which rises into the air. At school we have a drinking **fountain** where we can get a drink.

North, South, East, and West are the **four** points on a compass.

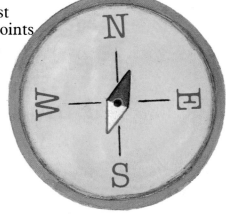

four (4)

Four is a number. There are **four** points on a compass.

free

1. When you are **free** you are able to do and move exactly as you please. The bird was set **free** from the cage.
2. **Free** also means that you do not have to pay any money. The theater seats were **free**.

freeze

If water gets very cold it will **freeze** and turn into ice. In winter, the water often **freezes** in the pond. When I played in the snow, my hands soon felt **frozen**. Feel my fingers – aren't they **freezing**?

fresh

Fresh food is newly picked or cooked. It is not old and stale. My Mom picked some **fresh** cabbage from the garden. This bread smells so delicious, it must be **fresh**.

Friday

Friday is the sixth day of the week. Most people finish work on **Friday** before the weekend. "**Friday's** child is loving and giving," says the rhyme.

friend

A **friend** is a person you like very much. My best **friend** and I share all our adventures. That dog has become very **friendly** since you started to feed it. The opposite of **friendly** is **unfriendly**.

frighten

Mary tried to **frighten** me. She tried to make me feel afraid. Don't be **frightened** of the dark.

frog

A **frog** is an animal that is born in water but which lives much of the time on land. Animals like this are called amphibians (am-fib-ians). **Frogs** have strong legs for jumping and swimming.

A **friendly**-looking frog.

front

The **front** of something is the part that faces forward. The opposite side to the **front** is the back.

frost

Frost is the powdery ice that covers things when it is very cold. On a cold day, **frost** often makes patterns on the window.

frown

When people are worried or thinking hard, they wrinkle their faces into a **frown**. Stop **frowning** and try to smile.

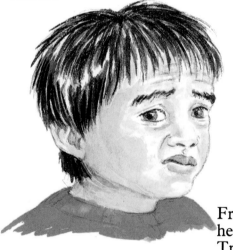

Our home is **furnished** with **furniture**.

Fred **frowns** when he is unhappy. Try to smile!

fruit

The **fruit** of a plant is the part that grows around the seed. **Fruit** is picked from bushes and trees when it is ripe. Many fruits are good to eat.

fry

Fry means to cook food in hot oil.

full

Her basket is **full** of apples. There is no space in it for any more. **Full** is the opposite of empty.

fun

When you're having a good time you're having **fun**. Jokes are **funny**. They make you laugh.

fur

An animal's hairy coat is called its **fur**. My cat has long black **fur**. It is **furry**.

furniture

Your home is full of **furniture**. **Furniture** is the name we give to such things as beds, tables, and chairs.

future

The **future** is that time yet to come. In the **future**, people may live in space.

Football and basketball are **games**.
Some people like to play a **game** of chess.

gallery

A **gallery** is a building where pictures and other kinds of art are shown.

gallon

A **gallon** is an amount of liquid. You can buy a **gallon** of gasoline for your automobile.

gallop

When a horse runs quickly, it **gallops**. I will **gallop** from one end of the field to the other on my horse.

game

Will you play a **game** of cards with me? A **game** is a way of playing. The two teams played a basketball **game**.

garage

A car is kept in a **garage**. Our **garage** is under the house. Put your bike in the **garage!**

garbage

Trash and waste are called **garbage**. The **garbage** is collected once a week.

garden

Some people have a **garden** in their backyard. A garden is a piece of land where flowers or vegetables are grown.

gas

Oxygen is a **gas**. Air is a mixture of oxygen and other **gases**. We breathe air. We burn a different **gas** to heat our food and homes.

gasoline

Gasoline is fuel for a car's engine. We fill our cars' **gas** tanks with **gasoline** at a gas station.

gate

A **gate** is an outside door. Close the garden **gate** or the dog will escape.

gentle

I gave the baby a **gentle** kiss. **Gentle** means kind or quiet.

get

To **get** means to receive. Can I **get** a ticket for the bus here? I am **getting** a ticket for you as well. Have we **got** the umbrella with us?

ghost

The spirit of a dead person said to haunt the earth is called a **ghost**. **Ghosts** are not real.

George is a **gentle giant**. He is closing the **gate** very **gently**. You can read about **giants** in fairy tales.

geography

People who study the earth and the way we live on it are studying **geography.**

giant

The huge man who was killed by Jack in "Jack and the Beanstalk" was a **giant**. There are **giants** in many fairy tales.

giraffe

A **giraffe** is an animal with a long neck and long legs. **Giraffes** live in Africa.

Giraffes are the tallest living animals. They are three times as tall as a very tall person.

girl

A **girl** is a young female. **Girls** grow up to be women.

give

When you **give** a present, you hand it over to someone. **Give** me a glass of lemonade, please. We **gave** our teacher a farewell present. She was **given** a present.

glad

Glad means pleased or happy. I am **glad** you came to my party.

glass

Many bottles are made of **glass**. **Glass** is strong and you can see through it. A **glass** is something you drink from. **Glasses** break easily when you drop them on the floor.

The team that scores the most **goals** wins the game.

glove

You wear **gloves** on your hands to keep them warm. **Gloves** have parts that cover each finger.

glue

Glue is a sticky liquid. You can join things together with **glue**.

gnome (nome)

I read a fairy tale about a little magic man called a **gnome**. Some people put model **gnomes** in their gardens.

go

If you **go** somewhere you move from one place to the other. Let's **go** to the beach after lunch. Is your watch still **going**? Is it still moving or working? He has **gone** to the hospital. Last year, I **went** to Switzerland.

goal

When the ball enters the net in a hockey game, it enters the **goal**. You score **goals** in lots of other games, too.

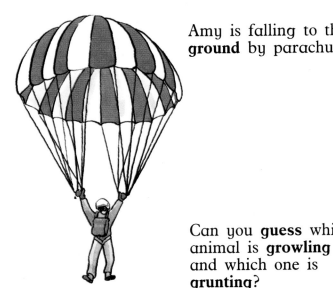

Amy is falling to the **ground** by parachute.

Can you **guess** which animal is **growling** and which one is **grunting**?

ground

The **ground** is the surface of the earth.

group

When several people meet together, they form a **group**. The class was divided into **groups** for the swimming lesson.

grow

1. When plants and animals **grow**, they become taller. Those trees are **growing** very high. They have **grown** higher than the house.
2. **Grow** can also mean to become. It **grew** dark as the clouds hid the sun.

growl

Dogs **growl** when they are angry. Tell your dog to stop **growling** at my cat.

grunt

Pigs **grunt**. A **grunt** is a short, deep sound.

guard

A **guard** is a person who protect something or someone. There are police on **guard** outside the White House in Washington. To **guard** means to protect.

guess

I didn't know the answer so I had to **guess**. When you **guess** you decide something without knowing if you are right or wrong.

guilty

Children are taught what is right and what is wrong. We feel **guilty** when we do something we shouldn't.

Tom is a **guitarist.** He plays the **guitar.**

Hh

guitar
A **guitar** is a musical instrument with six strings. A musician makes notes by touching the strings with his fingers.

gum
1. The flesh which holds your teeth in your mouth is called your **gum.**
2. **Gum** is also a rubbery mixture that is flavored and good to chew. I like strawberry chewing **gum.**

gun
A **gun** is a thing that shoots bullets. The outlaw pulled out his **gun** and shot the sheriff.

gym (jim)
Gym is short for **gymnasium.** Athletes do exercises called **gymnastics** in a **gym.**

had See **have.**

hair
Hair grows on your skin. All mammals have **hair** on their bodies. A dog has more **hair** than a seal.

half (haf)
When something is cut into two parts that are the same size, each part is a **half.** Put together two **halves** to make a whole.

Half an apple. Two **halves** make a whole.

Halloween

The festival of **Halloween** is celebrated on October 31. We like to put on costumes and go "trick-or-treating" on **Halloween.**

hamburger

A flat cake made of chopped beef is a **hamburger. Hamburgers** are eaten in a **hamburger** bun with ketchup and onions.

handle

He picked up the cup by its **handle.** The **handle** is the part of an object used for lifting it.

hang

Hang out your wet clothes to dry. My father is **hanging** new pictures on the living room wall. She **hung** her dress on a hook.

The wet clothes are **hanging** on the line to dry.

hammer

A tool which hits nails into wood is called a **hammer**. It has a long handle. The man **hammered** the nails into the fence.

Hamsters eat fruit and leaves.

hamster

A **hamster** is a small, mouselike animal. **Hamsters** fill their cheeks with food.

happen

When something takes place, it **happens.** What has **happened** in school today?

happy

When you feel cheerful and good about something, you are **happy**. We wish you a **happy** birthday!

hard

1. Something that is firm to touch is **hard. Hard** is the opposite of soft.
2. **Hard** can also mean not easy to do. It's **hard** to learn to skate.

91

My Uncle Nick is driving a combine **harvester**. It cuts and gathers the wheat when it is ripe.

harvest

When the fruit or vegetable crops are ripe and are gathered up, the **harvest** is taking place. In autumn we **harvest** the apples and pears.

hat

A **hat** is worn on the head to keep it warm and dry. There are lots of different **hats**.

hate

You may **hate** anything you really do not like. I **hate** to eat spinach.

have

You **have** a thing that is yours. Do you **have** a bicycle of your own? Yes, I **had** a small one when I was younger.

he

Nick is a boy. **He** is a boy. **His** name is Nick. Give Nick an apple. Give **him** an apple.

head

Your **head** is the top part of your body. Your face and hair are part of your **head**.

hear

When you listen, you **hear** noises. Sounds are **heard** through your ears.

heart

Your **heart** is in your chest. It sends blood around the body. When I went into the dark woods my **heart** started to beat very fast.

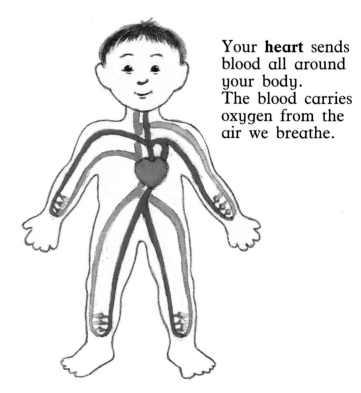

Your **heart** sends blood all around your body. The blood carries oxygen from the air we breathe.

heat

Heat is given off by hot things. The sun **heats** the earth.

heaven

Christians believe that they will go to **heaven** when they die.

heavy

Things that weigh a lot are **heavy**. My schoolbag is too **heavy** to lift.

heel

The rounded part at the back of your foot is called the **heel**.

Instead of wings like an airplane, **helicopters** have spinning blades called rotors. **Helicopters** can move in any direction.

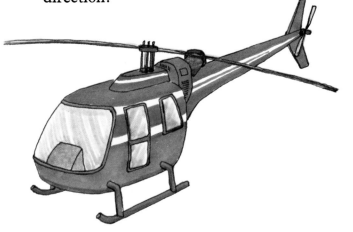

held See **hold**.

helicopter

A **helicopter** is a machine that flies. It is lifted into the air by spinning blades.

hello

I say **hello** to everyone I know when I see them in the street. They sometimes say "hi" instead of **hello** to me.

helmet

A **helmet** is a hard hat which keeps your head from getting hurt. Don't go into the cave without putting on your **helmet**.

help

When you **help** someone, you do something that they find useful. **Help** me clean your bedroom! Bill **helped** the old lady carry her bags.

hen

A **hen** is a female bird. **Hens** lay eggs that we eat for breakfast.

A mother **hen** and her chicks.

93

Skyscrapers are **high** buildings.

Which is the **highest** skyscraper in the picture?

here

Here is the place nearest to me. Come **here** and let me whisper a secret. Put the book **here** so that I can read it.

hibernate

Some animals go to sleep when the weather gets cold in winter. We say that they **hibernate**. My tortoise **hibernates** in a warm box.

hide

Hide the chocolate or the dog will eat it. When you **hide** something, you put it in a place where it cannot be seen. He **hid** behind a tree. Where have you **hidden** my toys?

high

High places are a long way from the ground. Skyscrapers are **high**, and so are mountains.

hill

A **hill** is a big bump in the ground. We climbed the **hill** to get a good view of the sea. The road through the mountains was very **hilly**.

The name **hippopotamus** means "river horse."

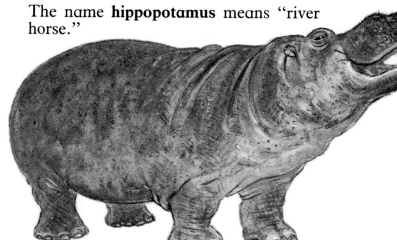

hippopotamus

The **hippopotamus** is a very big animal that spends a lot of its time in water. Its body is heavy. It finds it difficult to walk on land.

history

Things that happened in the past are **history**. We learned about the Incas in a **history** lesson.

hit

When you **hit** a ball you strike it. **Hit** the nail with the hammer.

hold

Hold my hand and you won't get lost. When you are **holding** something, you have it in your hands. Eliza **held** Jim's hand.

hole

A hollow place is called a **hole**. Squirrels sleep in a **hole** in a tree. I have **holes** in my shoes.

hollow

A **hollow** thing has empty space inside. This dead tree is completely **hollow**.

home

Your **home** is where you live. I am going **home** to feed my hamster.

honest

An **honest** person always tells the truth.

honey

Honey is a sweet, golden liquid made by bees. I eat **honey** on bread.

hoof

The foot of a horse is called a **hoof**. Many animals that eat grass have **hooves**.

hook

A **hook** is a bent piece of metal. I hang my clothes on a **hook**.

hop

When you jump on one foot, you **hop**. I won the **hopping** race.

hope

When you want something to happen, you **hope** it will happen. I **hope** the sun will shine tomorrow.

horn

A **horn** is a pointed part on an animal's head. A rhinoceros has a large curved **horn** on its nose.

The **home** of a bee is called a hive. Bees make **honey** in their hives.

horse

A **horse** is an animal used for riding. **Horses** have four legs and can gallop very fast.

hose

A **hose** is a long pipe that carries water. The water from the **hose** soon put out the fire.

hospital

Sick people are taken to the **hospital** to be made well. The doctor took an X ray of my knee at the **hospital.**

hot

Hot things are very warm to touch. In the summer the sun feels **hot**.

hot dog

A **hot dog** is something to eat. It is long and round and filled with meat and eaten on a bun with mustard.

hotel

You can eat and sleep in a **hotel** when you are away from home. You must pay for a bedroom in a **hotel**.

hour

An **hour** lasts for sixty minutes. Each day has twenty-four **hours**.

house

Houses are buildings. My family lives in a **house**. We have four rooms in our **house**.

how

How asks a question. It asks the way in which something happens. **How** is a snowflake made? **How** are you? Are you well?

howl

A **howl** is a long, sad crying noise. The child **howled** with anger when its toy was taken away.

huge

Very big things are **huge**. The Sphinx is a **huge** statue.

Every **hour** the clock strikes. *The clock struck one, the mouse ran down, hickory, dickory dock.*

human

People are **human**. Men, women, and children are all **human** beings.

hump

Some camels have two **humps** on their backs. A **hump** is a rounded lump or bump.

hundred

A **hundred** is also written 100. Ten times ten equals a **hundred**.

hurry

To **hurry** means to do something quickly. Don't **hurry** your homework or you will make mistakes. I **hurried** home after school on my birthday.

hungry

When you need something to eat you feel **hungry**. In winter we feed the **hungry** birds.

hunt

To **hunt** means to look for or to chase something so that you can catch it or kill it. People who **hunt** are called **hunters**. The detective **hunted** all over the park for a clue.

The sphinx is a very, very big statue in Egypt. It is **huge**. It has the head of a man and the body of a lion.

hurt

A person who is **hurt** will have some kind of injury. Have you **hurt** your arm playing basketball?

husband

The man who marries a woman is called her **husband**.

ice

When water freezes it is called **ice**. **Ice** is cold and hard.

iceberg

An **iceberg** is a large floating block of ice. Only the tip of the **iceberg** appears above the surface of the sea.

ice cream

Ice cream is a delicious food. **Ice cream** is made with frozen cream and sugar, and juice to add flavor.

idea

Bob suddenly had an **idea** about how to earn more pocket money. His **idea** was a thought.

if

When a sentence starts with **if**, it shows that something may or may not happen. **If** it stops snowing, we can go out. **If** the bus comes on time, I won't be late for school.

Most of an **iceberg** is hidden under the sea.

igloo

Eskimos build a house of ice blocks. It is called an **igloo**.

ill

Jane is not feeling well. She is **ill**.

important

If something is **important**, it matters a lot. She is an **important** person in the bank.

in

In describes the place inside. There is a teabag **in** my cup.

include

I want to **include** my poem in this poetry collection. To **include** something means to make it part of a group or collection.

Indian

An **Indian** is a person who was born and lives in India.

An **Indian** is also a person from one of the tribes that were in America before the Europeans arrived.

ink

Ink is a colored liquid that is used in pens for writing. The teachers put a cross in red **ink** by all my answers.

insect

An **insect** is a small animal with six legs. Bees, ants, and grasshoppers are all **insects**.

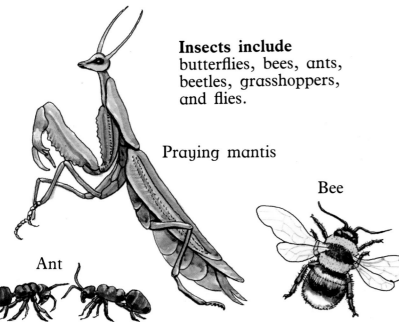

Insects include butterflies, bees, ants, beetles, grasshoppers, and flies.

Praying mantis

Bee

Ant

inside

If you are **inside** the house, you are not outside. You are indoors. **Inside** means the same as in or within.

into

If you enter a room, you go **into** it. Put the knife **into** the drawer.

invisible

You cannot see **invisible** things. Fairies must be **invisible**, because I've never seen one!

invite

When you **invite** people, you ask them to visit you. Jane **invited** her friends to her birthday party.

iron

1. **Iron** is a hard metal. **Iron** is used to make steel. Many tools are made from steel.
2. When we **iron** clothes we press the creases out of them.

island

An **island** is a piece of land surrounded by water. Greenland is a large **island**. The West Indies are a group of **islands** near America.

The sea is all around this **island**.

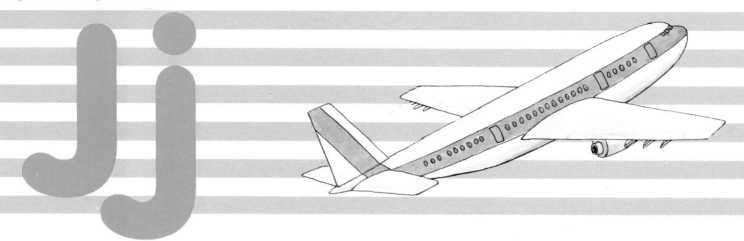

Jj

jacket
A **jacket** is a short coat.

jaguar
A **jaguar** is a member of the wild cat family. The coat of a **jaguar** is golden with black markings.

January
The New Year starts on **January** 1. January is the first month of the year.

jealous
I am **jealous** of Sue because she has dancing classes and I don't. You may feel **jealous** of people who have something you want.

jet
A **jet** travels at great speed through the air. **Jet** planes have **jet** engines.

jewel
A pretty stone that costs a lot is a **jewel.**

A **jet** is a kind of aircraft. It has a **jet** engine which drives the airplane forward by pushing gases backward.

join
When you place a number of things together you **join** them. We all **joined** hands in a circle.

joint
Where two parts meet is called a **joint.** The knee is the **joint** between the upper and lower bones of the leg.

joke
A story or saying that makes people laugh is called a **joke.** The comedian told **jokes** on the television.

juice
The liquid that can be squeezed out of food is called **juice.** Oranges contain a lot of **juice.** Carrot **juice** is good for you, too.

Kk

July

In **July** the weather is hot in one part of the world and cold in the other. **July** is the seventh month of the year.

jump

When you leap in the air with both legs, you **jump**. Jack **jumped** over the stream, but he didn't fall in.

June

June is the sixth month of the year. In many parts of the world, roses bloom in **June**.

jungle

A **jungle** is a thick forest of trees and bushes. **Jungles** grow in hot, damp countries. The Amazon River in South America, flows through a hot **jungle**.

Kangaroos use their strong back legs to **jump**. Their long tails help them to **keep** their balance.

kangaroo

A **kangaroo** is a strange kind of animal that carries its baby in a pouch or pocket on its front. **Kangaroos** live in Australia. They have strong back legs which they use for jumping.

keep

When you hold something in one place, you **keep** it there. We **keep** tools in the tool box. Are you **keeping** this old bike or can I throw it away? I **kept** my hamster in a cage, but it escaped.

A dog's house is called a **kennel**.

kennel

A place where dogs are kept is a **kennel**.

key

A **key** is a special tool that opens and closes the lock on a door. I lost my **keys** and couldn't open the door.

Nick always **kicks** a ball with his right foot.

kick

When you hit something hard with your foot, you **kick** it. He **kicked** the ball right over the goal post.

kid

Kid is a word people sometimes use instead of child. Would you **kids** like to go to the circus?

kill

If something causes a person to die, we say it kills them. A falling rock can **kill** you. Many people are **killed** in highway accidents.

kind

1. What **kind** of car shall we buy? What **kind** means the same as what sort or type.
2. **Kind** also means gentle. She was very **kind** to her sick kitten.

kindergarten

Young children go to **kindergarten** before they go to school. **Kindergarten** is a German word that means "children's garden."

king

Many countries used to be ruled by a **king**, but today there are few **kings**. The wife of a **king** is a queen, and their children are princes and princesses.

kitchen

The **kitchen** is the room in a house where food is cooked.

knee (nee)
The bending joint in your leg is your **knee**. Each time I fall over I bruise my **knees**.

kneel (neel)
When you **kneel** you place your knees on the ground. Some people **kneel** down to say their prayers.

knife (nife)
A **knife** is a cutting tool. It has a sharp blade which slices through things. You must be very careful how you pick up **knives**.

knock (nok)
Go and **knock** at the front door. When you beat on a hard surface with your hand, you are **knocking**. Our dog **knocked** the cake off the table.

knot (not)
I can't undo the **knot** in my ribbon. We tie **knots** to join two pieces of string or ribbon together tightly. How many **knots** do you know?

know (no)
The things that you **know** are those you understand. I **know** all your secrets. If I had **known** it was raining, I would have brought an umbrella. I **knew** you were in the kitchen.

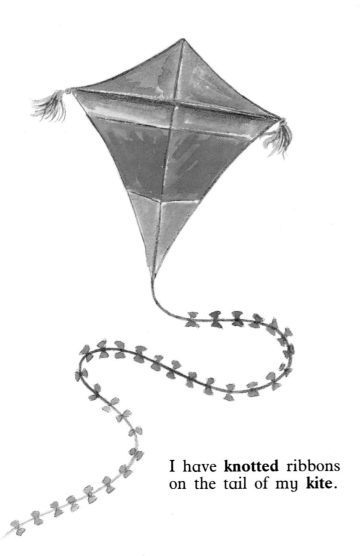

I have **knotted** ribbons on the tail of my **kite**.

kite
Joe flew his **kite** high in the air. A **kite** is a toy that is lifted in the air by the wind. It is made of paper or cloth stretched over a cross frame.

kitten
A baby cat is called a **kitten**. **Kittens** like to play with string.

A **lamb** is a baby sheep.

ladder

A **ladder** is a set of steps that you can carry around. You climb a **ladder** to reach high places.

lake

A large stretch of water that has land around it is called a **lake**. The boat sailed from one side of the **lake** to the other.

lamb

A mother sheep gives birth to a **lamb**. **Lambs** are usually born in the spring.

land

1. The sailors were happy to see **land**. The part of the earth that is not covered by water is called **land**.
2. When planes come down at the airport, they **land**.

language

The people who live in Spain speak the Spanish **language**. The way in which we talk is called our **language**.

large

Large things are not small. Bob is wearing a hat that is too **large**.

lasso

A **lasso** is a long rope used by cowboys to catch cattle.

We are sailing in the middle of a **large lake**. Look at the **land** over there.

last

The **last** person in line is the one at the end. The **last** month of the year is December.

late

If you arrive **late**, you arrive after you are expected. The bus is half an hour **late**.

laugh (laaf)

We **laugh** at funny things. When we **laugh**, we open our mouths and make a noise like ha-ha-ha. We **laughed** at the clowns in the circus.

launch

A rocket is **launched** into space from the **launch** pad and flies at great speed through the air.

law

A **law** is a rule made by the government of a country. The **law** tells you what you can do and you can't do. The person who steals is breaking the **law**.

lay

1. **Lay** the papers on my desk. To **lay** is to put something down in a careful way.
2. Hens **lay** eggs. Have they **laid** some today?

lazy

Lazy people don't want to work. Tim's so **lazy** he never gets out of bed until lunchtime.

lead

1. **Lead** (rhymes with reed). **Lead** me to the hidden cave. When you **lead** someone you go ahead of them to show them the way.
A **leader** is a person who acts as guide.
2. **Lead** (rhymes with bed). **Lead** is a kind of metal that bends easily.

leaf

A **leaf** is a green part of a plant. In the fall, some trees lose their **leaves**.

lean

1. **Lean** people are slim. **Lean** meat is meat with no fat.
2. **Lean** also means to put in a sloping position. Dick **leaned** the ladder against the wall.

"Go on Dan, you **lead** the way. I'll follow you."

learn

People who **learn** their lessons know lots of useful facts. Today we **learned** the two times multiplication table.

leather

Leather is made from the skin of an animal. I am wearing **leather** shoes.

leave

When you **leave** something, you go away. Will you **leave** me alone? He is **leaving** the house now. He **left** at four o'clock.

left

Left is the opposite of right. Go **left** at the next corner.

leg

Your **leg** is a part of your body. You have two **legs**. The dancer kicked a **leg** up in the air.

lemon

The **lemon** is a sour-tasting fruit. **Lemons** are yellow.

lend

Will you **lend** me your bicycle? Will you let me have the use of your bicycle for a short while? She **lent** me a dress for the party. I borrowed her dress.

leopard

A **leopard** is a wild member of the cat family. **Leopards** have spotted coats.

less

He has **less** money than I do. He doesn't have as much money as I do.

lesson

A **lesson** is a period when you learn something. Children have **lessons** in school. Today I have a piano **lesson**.

let

To **let** means the same as to allow. **Let** me have a ride in your car. **Let's** means "**let** us."

I have written a **letter** to Mary.

letter

1. A **letter** is a written message from one person to another. Send your grandmother a thank-you **letter** for your present.

2. A **letter** is also a part of the alphabet. D, E, F, and G are **letters**.

library

A collection of books is kept in a **library**. I borrowed a book to read from the school **library**. We have two **libraries** in our town.

lick

To **lick** is to taste with your tongue. I **licked** all the chocolate off the biscuit. My dog likes to try and **lick** me.

lid

A **lid** is the top part of a container. Put the **lid** on the box. Can you get the **lid** off this bottle?

lie

1. People **lie** down when they wish to rest. They put themselves down flat. **Lie** on the bed and go to sleep. The cat is **lying** on the cushion.
2. When people don't tell the truth, they **lie**. He was **lying** about the result of the experiment. He **lied** to the policewoman.

life

The **life** of a person begins at birth and ends at death. A cat is said to have nine **lives**. All living things have life.

lifeboat

A **lifeboat** is a strong boat used for saving people at sea.

Bob is big and strong. He can **lift** very heavy weights.

lift

When you **lift** something you raise it. The wind **lifted** the kite up into the air.

My brother Ben is tired. He is resting. He is **lying** in his chair asleep.

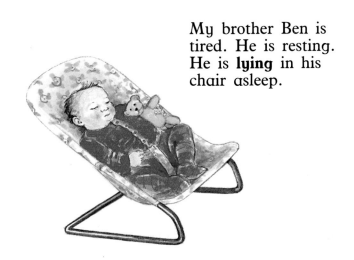

light

1. Light is given off by the sun and by lamps. Turn on the **light** so we can see our way.

2. Light also means not heavy. Feathers are **light**.

Lighthouses have bright **lights**. The **lights** tell ships that there are dangerous rocks in the sea.

lighthouse

A **lighthouse** is a tall building at sea or near the coast. The light from the **lighthouse** warns ships of dangerous rocks.

lightning

During a storm, you can sometimes see a quick flash of light in the sky. This is **lightning**. The noise of thunder follows the **lightning**.

Lucy **likes** playing with her toys.

like

1. I **like** all my toys. I enjoy playing with them. I **like** people I enjoy spending time with.

2. If one thing is **like** another, they are similar. Tom is just **like** his twin sister.

line

A **line** is a long, thin mark. Some **lines** are straight and some are curved.

When you see **lightning**, listen for thunder.

lion

A **lion** is a large wild animal of the cat family. Around its neck a **lion** has a lot of fur called a mane. **Lions** live in Africa.

lip

The fleshy part on the top and bottom of your mouth is called a **lip**. She kept her **lips** tightly together and wouldn't say a word.

liquid (lick-wid)

A liquid is wet. Water is a liquid. Milk is a liquid. Liquids flow.

listen (liss-en)

People **listen** when they wish to hear something. **Listen** to the music.

little

Little things are not very big. Babies are **little** when they are born.

live

I **live** in a town. My home is in a town. Most plants and animals cannot **live** in the desert.

liver

The **liver** is inside your body. Your **liver** helps your body use food.

lock

You **lock** a door by turning a key in a **lock** When the door is **locked** you cannot open it.

long

My school is a **long** way from my house. The distance between them is very great. Susie has **long** hair. **Long** things are not short.

look

We **look** at things with our eyes. **Look** at the time on the clock. Mike **looked** both ways before he crossed the street.

Look both ways before you cross a street.

loose (loos)

Something that is **loose** is not fixed in one place. Harry had a **loose** tooth. The dogs ran **loose** in the park.

109

lose (looz)

When you **lose** something you cannot find it. Are you **losing** your way? The travelers were **lost** in the jungle.

lot

I have a **lot** of apples. I have many of them.

loud

A **loud** noise is a strong one. The man with the trumpet blew a long, **loud** note. **Loud** is the opposite of quiet.

love

If you **love** someone, you care a lot about them. I **love** my mother and father.

low

A **low** place is one that is not high up. It is near the ground. Put the dish on the **low** shelf.

lump

A **lump** is a bump. Nick has a **lump** on his head where the ball hit him. Please put some **lumps** of coal on the fire.

machine

A **machine** helps us do work. We use **machines** in the home to help us sew, cook, and clean. We clean the floor with an electric **machine** that sucks up dust. An oven is a **machine** that heats food.

A mechanic is mending the **machine**. **Machines** are made of parts that move. Mechanics know how **machines** work.

magic

Fairies are said to perform **magic** when they cast spells. Witches make evil **magic**. Can you do a **magic** trick?

magnet

A **magnet** is able to make iron and steel cling to it. You can use a **magnet** to pick up pins.

Mary is picking up pins with a **magnet**. **Magnets** are made of metal.

magnifying glass

A **magnifying glass** is a special kind of glass that you look through. It makes things seem larger.

make

If you **make** something, you build it or put it together. **Make** a cake for tea! What are you **making** with that wood? He **made** a painting of the sea.

male

Men and boys are **male**. **Male** is the opposite of female.

mammal

A **mammal** is an animal that feeds its young with milk from its body. Elephant are **mammals**. So are mice and whales.

man

A **man** is a male. When boys grow up they become **men**.

many

Many means a lot. I have **many** toys. **Many** people dream when they are asleep.

map

A **map** is a plan of an area. The driver needed a **map** of the city. Without a **map**, we got lost in the mountains.

Can you see it on the **map**?

march

To **march** means to step in time to a beat. The soldiers **marched**, left, right, left, right.

111

March
March is the third month of the year.

mark
A **mark** is a dark spot or some kind of written sign. You have a black **mark** on your shirt. He **marked** the paper with a cross.

marry
When a man and woman become husband and wife, they **marry**. When my sister **marries**, there will be a big wedding. My parents were **married** in a church.

A **mask** can be made from many **materials**. This **mask** is made of paper.

mask
People can change the way they look by wearing a **mask**. A **mask** is a cover for the face. Face **masks** are sometimes very ugly.

match
1. If two things **match**, they look alike or go together. Does the color of this hat **match** the color of my coat?

2. A small thin piece of wood with a special substance at one end. When this end is rubbed against something else it makes a flame.

material
Material describes what something is made of. Cotton is a **material**. My skirt is made of soft **material**.

May
May is the fifth month of the year.

meal
When you sit down to eat, you are having a **meal**. Breakfast, lunch, and supper are **meals**. Lunch is my favorite **meal** of the day.

mean
1. If you **mean** to do something, you plan to do it. I was **meaning** to telephone you, but I forgot. I **meant** to go to school today, but I had a cold.

2. A person who is not friendly and nice is mean. **Mean** children are often unkind.

3. You also use the word **mean** when you want to say two things are the same. "Small" means "little."

measure
To **measure** means to find out how much there is. **Measure** the distance from here to there.

meat

Meat is the flesh of an animal. Beef is the **meat** of a cow. Animals that eat **meat** are called "carnivores." Roast lamb is my favorite **meat**.

medicine

When you are sick, you take **medicine** to help you get better. Cough **medicine** helps you get better.

meet

When you **meet** your friends, you come face to face with them. I am **meeting** my mother in the restaurant. I **met** a sailor on the ship.

Slices of **melon**.

melon

A **melon** is a large, juicy fruit with a thick skin. If you are thirsty on a hot day, eat a slice of **watermelon**.

melt

Ice cubes turn to water as they **melt**. Ice cream **melts** in the hot sun.

mend

I broke my cart but was able to **mend** it with a nail. Broken things need **mending** so they will work again.

mess

Things that are very untidy are in a **mess**. After dinner, the kitchen was very **messy**.

message

You can send a **message** to tell somebody something. I sent John a note to say I would be late. Please tell Eric his supper is ready. If you see him, give him this **message**.

metal

Metal things are hard and strong. Iron, steel, and tin are all **metals**.

All these things are made of **metal**.

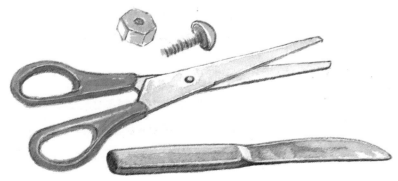

microscope

A **microscope** contains a special piece of glass called a lens. Tiny things appear larger when you see them through the lens of a **microscope**.

middle

The **middle** is another word for the center. Divide this cake down the **middle**.

midnight

A day ends at **midnight**. Twelve o'clock at night is **midnight.**

milk

We get **milk** from cows and goats. Beat together **milk** and ice cream to make a **milk**shake.

million

A **million** is written like this: 1,000,000. A **million** is one thousand multiplied by one thousand.

minute

A **minute** lasts sixty seconds. The water will boil in just three **minutes**. There are sixty **minutes** in an hour.

mirror

A **mirror** is a piece of glass that you look in to see yourself. The wicked queen asked the **mirror** who was the fairest in the land.

miss

1. When you do not hit or catch something, you **miss** it. Eric swung his bat, but **missed** the ball.
2. **Miss** can also mean to be sad because someone is not with you. I **missed** my sister when she was away.

mistake

Jim got the wrong answer to the problem. He made a **mistake**. Is it possible to **mistake** a chimpanzee for a gorilla?

Mandy looks at herself in the **mirror**.

mix

Mix the red paint with the yellow paint. Put the colors together. If you **mix** blue and yellow, you will get green.

Monday

Monday is the second day of the week. "**Monday's** child is fair of face," says the old rhyme.

money

Money is made up of coins and paper bills. I keep my **money** in a safe place.

monkey

A **monkey** is an animal that lives in the trees. **Monkeys** use their long arms, legs, and tails to swing through the trees.

month

The year is divided into twelve **months**. The **months** of the year are January, February, March, April, May, June, July, August, September, October, November, December.

Monkeys have hands and feet, which they use for climbing.

January
February
March
April
May
June
July
August
September
October
November
December

moon

The **moon** spins around our earth. We see the **moon** when it reflects the light of the sun. The sea shone in the **moonlight**.

more

I have **more** marbles than Tim. I have a larger number of marbles than him.

morning

The sun rises in the **morning**. We get up in the **morning**. **Morning** is the early part of the day.

mosque

People who are Muslims worship in a building called a **mosque**.

mosquito

A **mosquito** is a flying insect. Female **mosquitoes** bite your skin.

Moths usually fly at night. Butterflies are seen in the daytime.

Mountains are very high parts of the land. They are much higher than the land around them.

moth

A **moth** is an insect that looks like a butterfly. **Moths** usually fly at night.

mother

Your **mother** is one of your parents. A woman who has children is a **mother**.

mountain

A **mountain** is a high, rocky peak. The highest **mountain** in the world is Everest.

mouse

A **mouse** is a small, wild animal. It is furry and has a long tail and sharp teeth. Some **mice** live near people on farms and in houses.

mouth

Your **mouth** is a part of your face. You open your **mouth** to take in food. You have teeth inside your **mouth** to bite the food, and a tongue to taste it. You also open your **mouth** to talk.

move

You can **move** in many different ways. You can jump or skip or run. Anything that travels from one position to another is **moving**.

much

Much means more than enough of something. You are making too **much** noise.

mud

Mud is soft, wet earth. There was **mud** all over the farmer's boots.

mug

A **mug** is heavier than a cup.

multiply

When you **multiply**, you make a number bigger. Six **multiplied** by two equals twelve.

muscle

A **muscle** is a strong, working part of your body. You need your **muscles** to lift things, or to move your body.

museum

A **museum** is a building where collections of interesting things are on view. I saw the skeleton of a dinosaur at the Natural History **Museum**.

mushroom

A **mushroom** is a kind of plant. **Mushrooms** are umbrella-shaped.

Some **mushrooms** are good to eat. Others are poisonous. Do not pick **mushrooms**.

music

The notes from **musical** instruments make a pleasant sound called **music**. I am learning to play the guitar in my **music** lessons.

Nn

nail

1. A **nail** is a small piece of metal that is used to hold pieces of wood together. **Nails** are hammered into place.
2. The hard parts at the ends of your fingers and toes are **nails**.

name

Each person is known by a **name**. Every thing has a **name**, too. My dog's **name** is Snapper.

Take care not to hit your **nail** when you hammer the **nail**!

nature

Nature is the name we give to the world of mountains and rivers, plants and animals, in which we live.

naughty (naw-tee)

A **naughty** child is one who does not behave well. Have you been **naughty** today?

The cat is creeping **near** the bird. It has **nearly** reached it. Look out, bird!

narrow

A **narrow** opening is not very wide. The street was too **narrow** for the truck to enter.

near

Something that is **near** is not far away. The cat is creeping **nearer** the bird.

I **need** knitting **needles** to knit a sweater. A **needle** you sew with has a hole for the thread at one end.

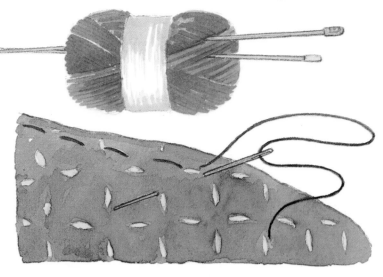

nearly

If something has **nearly** happened, it has almost taken place. I have **nearly** finished. I will finish in a moment.

neat

Things that are clean and have been placed where they are supposed to be are **neat**. My sister always keeps things **neat**, but I do not.

neck

Your **neck** is the part of your body that joins your head to your shoulders. She wore a necklace around her **neck**.

need

Things you **need** are things you must have. I **need** something to eat. When Sally fell down, she **needed** three stitches in her forehead.

needle

A **needle** is a thin, pointed piece of metal with a hole, called an eye, at one end. We use **needles** for sewing.

neighbor

Someone who lives near you, is your **neighbor**. My dog is in our **neighbor's** yard.

neither

Neither of those boxes is the right size. **Neither** Ronnie nor Bill is tall enough to reach the basket. **Neither** means not one nor the other.

nephew

The son of your sister or brother is your **nephew**.

nest

A bird makes a **nest** to hold its eggs. American robins build **nests** that look like cups made of mud and twigs.

Nests are birds' homes.

119

Becky used a **net** to catch fish.

net

A **net** is made of pieces of string that are knotted very loosely. Fish are trapped in the **net** when it is dragged through the water.

never

Things that **never** happen, do not happen at any time. You will **never** beat me at swimming.

new

New means just made. My sister bought a **new** car when her old car could not be mended.

newspaper

A **newspaper** is a printed sheet of paper that tells you what is happening in the world. My uncle buys the **newspaper** every day.

next

The doctor called the **next** person into her office. **Next** means the one that comes after. **Next** week is a holiday.

niece

A **niece** is the daughter of a brother or sister.

night

At **night**, we don't see the sun's light. It is dark. We go to bed at **night**.

By **nine** o'clock at **night** I am fast asleep.

nine (9)

Nine **is a number.**

no

1. There are **no** apples in the box. The box is empty. There are **none**.

2. You say **no** when you don't want to take or do something. The opposite of **no** is yes.

I opened the door, but **nobody** was there.

nobody
Nobody means the same as no person or no one. I heard footsteps, but **nobody** was there.

noise
Noise is the sound you hear. The people cheered and shouted and made a loud **noise**.

noon
Noon is twelve o'clock in the middle of the day. **Noon** is midday.

north
North is a direction. **North** is the opposite direction of south.

We smell flowers with our **noses**.

nose
The **nose** is the part of your face you use for breathing and for smelling. Most animals have **noses**.

not
Eric is **not** coming to my party. He is staying at home.

nothing
If you do not have anything, you have **nothing**. If a box is empty, there is **nothing** inside.

notice
A **notice** is a sign that you can read. Read the names of the winners on the **notice** board.

November
November is the eleventh month of the year.

now
Something that is happening **now** is happening at this time. Would you like to see my pet snake **now** or later?

nowhere

My hamster is **nowhere** in sight. I cannot see it anywhere.

number

A **number** is a word that says how many–5, 6, and 7 are **numbers**. I have a **number** of friends in Detroit. Think of a large **number** and I will try to guess it. The pages of the book are **numbered**.

nurse

A **nurse** takes care of you in the hospital. I **nurse** my dolls when they are ill.

nut

A **nut** is a hard shell with a fruit or seed inside. A **coconut** has a hard, hairy shell.

oak

The **oak** is a tall, wide-spreading tree. The seed of the **oak** tree is called an acorn.

oasis

An **oasis** is a place in a desert where plants grow because water is found there.

Deserts are very dry. An **oasis** has water.

This is an **old**-fashioned car. It was made over 100 years ago.

ocean

The large area of water between continents is called the **ocean**. The Pacific **Ocean** and the Atlantic **Ocean** are the two largest **oceans** in the world.

o'clock

When we look at the clock to tell the time, we use the word **o'clock**. I go to bed at eight **o'clock** at night.

October

October is the tenth month of the year.

odd

Any number that cannot be divided by two is an **odd** number–3, 5, and 7 are **odd** numbers.

off

Switch **off** the light. Take **off** your hat.

offer

Offer means that you say you will do something for somebody. I **offered** to help my aunt clean her car.

often

Something that happens **often**, happens over and over again. I **often** go to the supermarket to shop.

oil

Oil is a thick liquid found among rocks in the ground. **Oil** is burned to drive engines and and is used to make plastics. You can also get **oil** from the seeds of plants.

old

A person who is **old** has lived for a long time. **Old** toys are toys you have had for some time. **Old** things are not new.

on

On shows the place where something is standing. The cat is **on** the shelf. **On** can also say when. I visited my cousins **on** Sunday.

one (1)

If something is by itself, there is just **one** of it.

onion

An **onion** is a strong-tasting vegetable. I like fried **onions** on a hot dog.

only

Jane was the **only** girl in the group. **Only** means there is just one of that kind.

open

If a door is **open** you can walk through it. You can pass into places or through **open** things. **Open** is the opposite of closed. Tim **opened** his present.

opposite

1. Something that is very different is the **opposite**. Black is the **opposite** of white.
2. **Opposite** also means on the other side of, or facing. Tim's house is **opposite** mine. This page is **opposite** the next page.

or

If you are deciding between two things, you take one thing **or** the other. Would you like a hamburger **or** a hot dog?

orange

An **orange** is a round fruit. **Orange** is also a color. **Orange** objects are the same color as an **orange**.

This picture of a Royal Canadian Mounted Policeman is the **only** picture on this page. On the page **opposite** there are three pictures.

ordinary

There is nothing special or different about something that is **ordinary**. Nothing unusual happened today. Today was **ordinary**.

ostrich

An **ostrich** is the largest kind of bird. **Ostriches** cannot fly.

other

Do you want to wear this dress or the **other** one? The **other** thing is not this thing. Don't play with these toys. Play with the **others**.

out

When you leave the inside of your house, you go **out**. The cat went **out** into the backyard. I looked **out** of the window. If you take something from inside, you take it **out**. Take that doll **out** of its box!

outside

Outside is the place that is not inside. Inside the house it is quiet, but **outside** it's noisy. I'm going to play **outside** in the park.

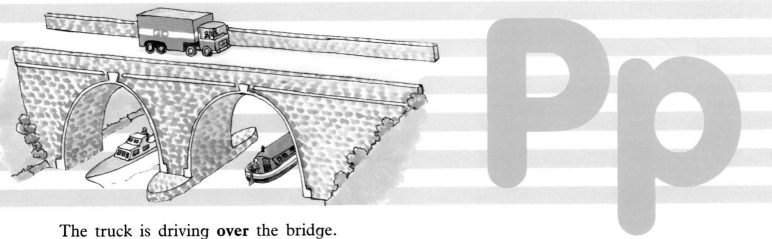

The truck is driving **over** the bridge.
The boats are sailing under the bridge.

over

Over means above. **Over** is the opposite of under. I hold an umbrella **over** my head so that I don't get wet. Today a balloon flew **over** our house.

owl

An **owl** is a large-eyed bird that hunts at night. It has a sharp, curved beak. **Owls** make a hooting cry.

own

You **own** something which belongs to you. I have a rabbit. I **own** it.

Owls go **out** at night to hunt.

pack

When we **pack** we put things into a container. We **packed** our clothes into a suitcase. The train is **packed**. It is full of people.

page

A **page** is one side of a piece of paper. Books and newspapers have **pages**.

pain

You feel **pain** when a part of your body is hurting. I ate so much for supper I had a **pain** in my stomach.

paint

1. Paint is a sticky colored liquid. Don't spill the **paint**!
2. Will you **paint** me a picture? When we **paint** we put colors on paper or objects.

125

pair

Two things that go together make a **pair**. A **pair** of birds landed on the fence. We wear a **pair** of socks and a **pair** of shoes.

A **pair** of socks. They are both the same size and the same color.

palace

The house of a king or queen is called a **palace**.

palm

1. A **palm** is a plant or tree that grows in warm countries. Dates and coconuts grow on a **palm**.
2. Your **palm** is the under part of your hand. You have lines that crisscross your **palm**.

pan

We cook eggs in a **pan**. A **pan** is a flat, metal pot that is used for heating food.

pancake

We fry a **pancake** in a pan. A **pancake** is a flat cake made from egg, flour, and milk.

The giant **panda** looks like a black and white bear.

panda

A **panda** is an animal that lives in China and looks like a bear. It has a black and white coat and feeds on bamboo shoots.

pants

People wear **pants** to cover the bottom part of their bodies and their legs. A suit is a matching jacket and pair of **pants.**

paper

We write on **paper**. Books are printed on **paper**. **Paper** is made from wood that has been chopped up and mixed with water, then rolled into thin sheets.

parachute

A **parachute** is a large round piece of cloth. When people jump out of a plane, their **parachutes** let them float down gently to earth.

parcel

A **parcel** is a box or container with things inside. My Mom received a large **parcel** for her birthday.

parent

Your mother is your **parent**. So is your father. I had a family photo taken with my **parents**.

park

1. A **park** is a large area of grass and trees where everyone is free to walk.
2. When you **park** the car, you stop beside the pavement or in the parking lot.

parrot

A **parrot** is a brightly colored bird that lives in warm countries. My **parrot** has learned to say "Pretty Polly."

part

Give me **part** of your pocket money. A **part** is a piece of something. Your arm is **part** of your body. Sue played the **part** of a fairy in the play.

party

A **party** is a group of people taking part in something together. Let's join the **party** going to the museum. On birthdays people have **parties**.

pass

To **pass** means to go ahead of. He **passed** me on his bicycle when I was climbing the hill.

Passover

Passover is a Jewish holiday.

past

Something which happened long ago happened in the **past**.

Parrots can be taught to talk.

path

A **path** is a way for walkers. There are flowers planted on either side of the **path**. They followed **paths** through the forest.

pattern

When shapes or colors are placed in a special way, they make a **pattern**. Do you like the **pattern** on my shirt?

Our cat hides her sharp claws in her soft **paws**.

paw

The foot of an animal with claws is called its **paw**. The hunter found the bear by following its **paw** marks in the snow.

pay

You **pay** money when you buy something. What did you **pay** for this hat? I **paid** too much for it.

pea

A **pea** is a green vegetable. The seeds of the pea plant are small, round **peas**.

peace

Peace describes a quiet feeling. It is a time when no one is fighting or arguing.

peach

A **peach** is a fruit. **Peaches** grow on trees in warm countries.

peanut

The seed of the **peanut** plant is good to eat. I ate a big bag of salted **peanuts**. Spread some **peanut** butter on the bread.

pear

A **pear** is a fruit that grows on trees.

pebble

Can you skim a **pebble** across the top of the water so that it bounces? **Pebbles** are small, smooth stones.

pedal

You **pedal** a bicycle to make the wheels turn around. The **pedals** are where you rest your feet.

peel

When you remove the skin from a fruit or vegetable, you **peel** it.

You can **peel** **peaches** and **pears** and apples. They have skins.

peep
I opened one eye and took a **peep**. When you **peep**, you take a quick look with half-open eyes.

pen
A **pen** is a writing tool. It is filled with ink. I write you a letter with my **pen**.

pencil
A **pencil** is a thin stick with "lead" inside it used for writing and drawing. Use colored **pencils** to fill in the shapes.

penguin
A **penguin** is a bird that swims but does not fly. **Penguins** dive into the sea to catch fish.

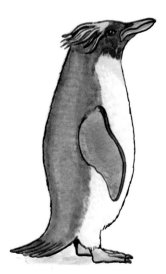

Penguins are birds that swim.

people
Men, women, girls, and boys are all **people**.

perhaps
Maybe it will happen. **Perhaps** it will happen. **Perhaps** the frog will turn into a prince.

person
A **person** is a human being. You are a **person**. Each **person** sat in a special place. All the **people** sat down to eat.

pet
If you keep an animal in your house, it is a **pet**. I have a **pet** snake.

Petals

petal
A **petal** is the soft, colored part of a flower. In the daytime the **petals** unfold.

photograph (foe-toe-graff)

You use a camera to take a **photograph**. I took a **photo** of the elephant. A **photo** is a copy of something you see.

piano

A **piano** is a musical instrument. It has wooden blocks called keys. When you press a key a hammer hits a piece of wire. This makes a musical note.

To play a **piano** you must press the keys.

pick

1. When you **pick** something up, you lift it. Dave **picked** up his bag.
2. **Pick** can also mean choose. Penny **picked** the yellow bicycle rather than the red one.

picnic

Pack a basket full of food to eat on a journey. Pack a **picnic** basket. We had our **picnic** on the beach.

picture

A **picture** is a drawing or painting. Frank painted a **picture** of a clown. Do you like the **pictures** in this book?

Who has taken a **piece** of **pie**?

pie

A **pie** is made with pastry. Pastry is made of flour and butter. Inside the pastry there is cooked fruit. Who would like a piece of blackberry **pie**?

piece

If you take a **piece** of something, you take a part of it. Would you like a **piece** of pie? When you make a jigsaw all the **pieces** fit together.

pig

A **pig** is a farm animal. It has a fat body and a short tail. A baby **pig** is called a **piglet**.

pile

A **pile** is the same as a heap. Who put that **pile** of bricks in my driveway?

130

pill

Sometimes you need to take a **pill** to make you feel better. Powdered medicines can be shaped into **pills**. **Pills** are pieces of medicine.

pillow

You rest your head on a **pillow** in bed. A **pillow** is a soft cushion.

pilot

A **pilot** flies an airplane. The **pilot** talked to the people during the flight.

pin

A **pin** is a small, sharp piece of metal that holds things together. The pieces of material were **pinned** together and then stitched.

pineapple

A **pineapple** is a fruit that grows in warm countries. **Pineapples** have long, pointed leaves and the fruit has sharp prickles.

Picking pineapples.

Pink is a color.

pink

Pink is a color. When you mix red with white you get **pink**. In the garden you can see **pink** roses and **pink** carnations.

pint

A **pint** is a measure of liquid. There are two pints in a quart.

place

1. When you **place** a cup on the table, you are putting it down. **Place** the sunbed in the shade.
2. Let's find a **place** where we can have a picnic. The **place** describes where something is. I've lost my **place** in the book.

plan

1. A **plan** is a drawing that shows the outline of a building or part of a building.
2. If you have a **plan**, you have an idea how to do something. I'm **planning** all kinds of games for my party.

planet

Earth is a **planet**. It is one of the nine **planets** that spin around the sun.

plant

A **plant** is a living thing that grows in one place and does not move. **Plants** take in food through their roots. Gardeners **plant** or place flowers in the earth. Penny **planted** a rosebush.

plastic

Plastic is a material made from oil. It can be made into many useful things. This chair is made of **plastic**. I put my groceries in a **plastic** bag.

We **play** outdoors in a **playground**.
Many **playgrounds** have swings and slides.

plate

A **plate** is a dish for holding food. Pass your **plate** and I'll give you some meat.

platform

A **platform** is like a small stage in a theater.

play

1. I'm sure you like to **play** with your friends. When you are **playing**, you have fun with games and sports.
2. You can go to the theater to watch a **play**. Actors and actresses take part in a **play**.

playground

A special place where children can play safely, is called a **playground**. Some **playgrounds** have swings and slides for young children.

please

Please is a word you should always use if you are asking for something. **Please**, may we have our ball back? People will be **pleased** to help you if you say **please**.

plow

A **plow** is a large tool that is pulled behind a tractor. **Plows** break up the soil into small pieces.

pocket

There is usually a flap on a coat or jacket in which you can place things. This is called a **pocket**.

poem

A **poem** can be a rhyme. Sometimes it is just a collection of ideas. **Poets** try to show how they feel about something in their **poetry**.

point

1. A pin has a sharp **point** at one end.
2. **Point** can also describe a way of using your fingers to show something. **Point** to the path that leads north.

poison

If you eat **poison** you will become very ill, and may even die. **Poison** is found in plants and some animals that can be dangerous to humans. Some snakes have a **poisonous** bite.

Some snakes have a **poisonous** bite.

Farmers turn over the soil with a **plow**. They **plow** fields.

pole

1. A **pole** is a long stick. Mom hung a washing line between two **poles**. Can you see the flag on the **flagpole**?
2. The North **Pole** and the South **Pole** are two points on the surface of the earth. There is lots of ice at the **Poles**.

police

The group of people who make sure that people obey the law is called the **police** force. A **policewoman** told us not to walk in the road.

polish

Polish is a kind of wax. You rub **polish** on a surface to make it shine. When you **polish** something you make it shine. Have you **polished** your shoes this week?

polite

It is **polite** to say "please" and "Thank you." **Polite** people behave well and try to help others.

133

pond

A **pond** is a small piece of water with land all around it. Ducks swim on the **pond** in the park.

pony

A **pony** is a small horse. Some children have **ponies** of their own to ride.

pool

We swim at the **pool**. A **pool** is a pond or a large bathing place.

poor

If you have very little money, you are **poor**. **Poor** people are not rich.

popular

Someone who is liked by everyone and who has many friends is **popular**. Nick is the most **popular** boy at our school.

population

Population is the number of people living in one place. What is the **population** of Mexico City?

pot

A **pot** is a kind of deep dish used for cooking. **Pots** have handles.

potato

The **potato** is a vegetable. **Potatoes** grow underground.

pound

A **pound** is sometimes written like this — lb. The weight of something is measured in **pounds**.

pour

Pour some milk for the cat. He **poured** water over my head. When liquid is **poured**, it is tipped out of its container.

powder

Powder is made when something is crushed into tiny, soft pieces. Flour is a **powder**. Do you put on talcum **powder** after a bath?

powerful

Something that is **powerful** is very strong. The car has a **powerful** engine.

present

A **present** is something you give to someone. Do you get **presents** on your birthday?

president

The person who is head of a government is sometimes known as a **president**. Italy, France, and the United States all have **presidents**.

Potatoes were first grown by South American Indians.

134

press

To **press** means to push down hard on something. We **pressed** our feet into the earth to leave deep footprints.

Pat is **pressing** a **potato print** onto the paper. She is **printing** a pattern onto the paper.

pretend

When you make-believe, you **pretend**. Dan and Miriam **pretended** to be ghosts.

pretty

Pretty things are nice to look at. Flowers are **pretty**.

prey

Animals that are hunted, killed, and eaten by other animals are prey. Chicken are the **prey** of foxes.

price

The amount of money you must pay to buy something is its **price**. What is the **price** of that pen?

prince

The son of a king is a **prince**. The sister of a **prince** is a **princess**.

print

To **print** means to press marks or patterns onto paper or material. Paper was **printed** with words and pictures to make this book. If you press your foot into wet sand, you will make a **footprint**.

prison

People who have done something very wrong may be sent to **prison** as a punishment. They are kept in a building and not allowed out.

prize

Rose won the **prize** for the best painting. The winners of competitions are often given **prizes**.

problem

It is difficult to find the answer to a **problem**. **Problems** are puzzling.

135

I **promise** to go to bed after my favorite TV **program**.

program

Did you watch the TV **program** about space machines? A **program** is a radio or television show.

promise

If you **promise** to do something, you say that you will surely do it. Pop **promised** to take us to the zoo today.

protect

To **protect** means to look after and keep from getting hurt. **Protect** your clothes from the rain by wearing a raincoat.

proud

If you are **proud** you feel especially good about something you have done. Pete felt **proud** of winning the race.

prove

Prove that you are brave by taking this spider out of the bathtub. When you **prove** something you show that it is true.

pudding

A **pudding** is something to eat. It is sweet and soft. Who'd like some more rice **pudding**?

puddle

The dip in the road filled up with rainwater and made a large **puddle**. **Puddles** are made when water cannot drain away.

A **puddle** filled with rainwater.

pull

When you **pull** you get hold of something and move it toward you or in the same direction as you. The donkey **pulled** the cart up the hill.

punch

If you hit someone with your fist, you **punch** that person.

punish

I will **punish** my dog if it keeps chasing cats. You may be **punished** if you do wrong. The **punishment** for being late is extra schoolwork.

pupil

A **pupil** is taught by a teacher. In my ballet class there are ten **pupils.**

A glove **puppet.**

puppet

A **puppet** is a doll that can be made to move. Some **puppets** are worked by pulling strings. Others are worn like a glove.

puppy

A **puppy** is a baby dog. **Puppies** must learn to behave while they are still young.

purple

You mix the colors red and blue to make **purple.**

purse

A **purse** is a handbag. People carry their money and small belongings in a **purse.**

push

To **push** is to move something away from you without lifting it. You **push** the door to go out.

put

When you **put** something down you place it. **Put** the knives away in the drawer. Have you **put** the car in the garage?

Wendy **put** a piece in the **puzzle.**

puzzle

A **puzzle** is a problem that is difficult to solve. Sometimes a **puzzle** has a trick answer.

Qq

The **queen** is sitting **quietly** next to the king. She is wearing a crown.

quack
Quack is the sound made by a duck.

quarrel
When people argue and become angry, they **quarrel**. The girls **quarreled** over who should push the baby carriage.

quarter
A **quarter** is a fourth part of something. In money, a **quarter** equals twenty-five cents. Four quarters equal one dollar.

A trot is **quick**, a canter is **quicker**, but a gallop is **quickest**.

Trot　　　　Canter　　　　Gallop

queen
A **queen** is a woman who rules a country. Sometimes a king and **queen** rule together. **Queen** Elizabeth is the **queen** of England.

question
When you ask about something to find out the answer, you are asking a **question**.

quick
Things done **quickly** take only a short time. We ran **quickly**.

quiet
Something that is **quiet** makes little or no noise. The countryside was peaceful and **quiet**.

quiz
A **quiz** is a short test in which questions must be answered.

Rr

Cycle **racing**.

rabbit

A **rabbit** lives in a burrow underground. It is a small, furry animal with a bobtail and long ears.

race

A **race** is a competition where drivers, athletes or animals try to see who is fastest. Danny won the auto **race** in his sports car. The horses **raced** around the track.

radio

You can listen to music and news programs on a machine called a **radio**.

railroad

A train runs on long strips of metal called **rails** – a **railroad**. The **railroad** leads from Chicago to Detroit.

rain

Rain is the water that clouds drop on the earth. When you see a **rainbow**, you see a band of color in the sky.

It **rained** yesterday and it is still **raining** today. It is **rainy** weather.

raise

If you **raise** something, you lift it up. Jan **raised** her arms above her head.

139

rattle

When something **rattles**, it shakes with a tapping sound. Babies play with a toy called a **rattle**.

Roger is **reaching** for the ball.

reach

When you **reach** a place, you arrive there. I **reached** the hotel by the sea. If you **reach** for something, you move part of your body towards it. I **reached** up to the shelf to take down a jar of honey.

read

You **read** a book. You look at the words in the book and understand what they mean.

ready

If you are **ready**, you are able to begin doing something. You have everything you need. Are you **ready** to eat supper? It's time you got **ready** for bed.

real

Things that are **real** are things you can believe in. Is that a **real** story or one you have made up? Things that are not **real** are make-believe.

record

1. You play a **record** when you want to listen to music. A **record** is a round piece of plastic with a hole in the middle. We put **records** on a **record player**.
2. A **record** is also the best that someone can do. Steve ran the race in **record** time.
3. A **record** can mean the story of an event. Your diary is a **record** of your life.

red

Red is a bright color. Many warning signs are **red** to catch your attention.

Danger! A tree has fallen. Wave a **red** flag.

refrigerator

A **refrigerator** is a box in which you keep food cool. Put the butter in the **refrigerator** so it won't melt.

remember

You **remember** things you don't forget. If you **remember** something you keep it in your mind. Bill **remembered** my birthday.

reply

When you **reply**, you answer. I am going to **reply** to this invitation. The prisoner **replied** that he had not done anything wrong.

rescue

If you **rescue** someone, you save that person. The lifeboat **rescued** the sailors from the sinking ship.

rest

1. You want to **rest** when you feel tired. The walkers sat on the grass and **rested**.
2. The **rest** is another word for those things that are left. The winners stood up and the **rest** sat down.

restaurant

You buy meals in a place called a **restaurant**. Someone brings food to your table in **restaurants**.

return

1. When you **return**, you come back. Andy **returned** to his home to see his mother.

2. **Return** also means to give something back. Jane **returned** the scarf I lent her.

Rhinos have very thick skins.

rhinoceros

A **rhinoceros** is sometimes called a **rhino**. It is a huge, strong animal that has a horn on top of its nose.

A **restaurant** is a place where you can buy meals. The food is brought to your table.

rhyme

When words **rhyme**, they share the same sound. "Care" **rhymes** with "hair." Some rhymes are poems.

ribbon

Jan wears her hair tied back with a **ribbon**. A **ribbon** is a long, narrow piece of colored material.

rice

Rice is a kind of grass plant. The seeds of the **rice** plant are cooked and eaten.

rich

Rich people have a lot of money. This man is so **rich** he doesn't know how much money he has.

ride

If a machine or animal carries you along, you **ride** on it. John **rides** a horse. I **rode** a bike to school yesterday. Have you ever **ridden** a horse or a bike?

right

1. Something that is **right** is correct. Is this the **right** way to get to the swimming pool? If something is not **right**, it is wrong.
2. At the corner, turn **right**, not left. In the picture at the top of the page the man dressed in blue is on the **right**.

Rice grows in fields filled with water. When it is **ripe** and ready to eat it is picked.

ring

1. A **ring** is a circle. The dancers held hands in a **ring**.
2. The bells in the church **ring** to call people to pray. The telephone **rang** for a long time. Has somebody **rung** the front doorbell?

ripe

A fruit that is soft and ready to eat is **ripe**. Don't eat apples that aren't **ripe**.

This man is **riding** a horse.

Tim's balloon is **rising** up into the air.

rise

When you stand up, you **rise**. The sun **rises** each morning. The rocket **rose** high in the sky.

river

A **river** is a large amount of moving water with land on both sides. It moves downwards from the hills to the sea. The Romans built bridges across **rivers**.

road

A **road** is a hard level path along which you drive cars and other vehicles. **Roads** are built between towns and villages.

roar

A **roar** is a loud noise made by engines, or by a fierce animal. The lion **roared** and sprang out of its cage.

roast

If you cook something in an oven or over a fire, you **roast** it. We **roasted** potatoes for supper.

rob

To **rob** means to take things that do not belong to you. The **robber** took money from the bank. He **robbed** the bank.

rock

1. To **rock** means to move something from side to side very gently. The boat **rocked** on the sea.
2. The earth is made of a hard material called **rock**. Mountains have steep **rocky** sides. Pieces of this material are called **rocks**.

rocket

A **rocket** is the name for a machine that is fired into space.

roll

Roll the ball along the ground. When something **rolls**, it turns over.

roller skate

A **roller skate** is a special shoe with wheels. It's easy to **roller skate**.

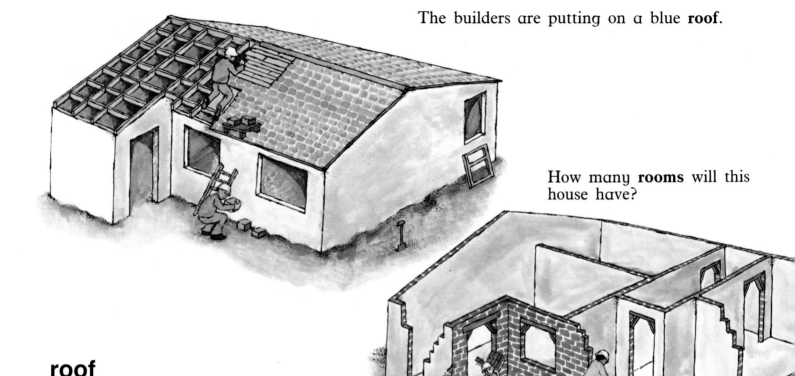

The builders are putting on a blue **roof**.

How many **rooms** will this house have?

roof

The top part of a building or vehicle is its **roof**. There is snow on the **roofs** of the houses. The car rolled over and landed on its **roof**.

room

A **room** is part of the inside of a building. My sister has a **workroom** where she does carpentry. My **bedroom** is full of toys.

root

The **root** of a plant is the part that fixes itself in the ground. A plant feeds itself through its **roots**.

rope

A **rope** is a strong length of cord. The boat was tied to the pole by a **rope**.

rose

A **rose** is a beautiful flower. You send a red **rose** to someone you love.

Cut the tops off the **roots** of the vegetable. Stand them in water and watch them grow.

rough

Something that feels **rough**, feels bumpy. My uncle's chin feels **rough** when he doesn't shave. The sea can be **rough** in a storm.

round

A **round** shape is one that looks like a circle or a ball. A full moon is **round**.

row (rhymes with go)

1. We placed the bottles on the shelf in a straight **row**. A **row** is a line. Trees are sometimes planted in **rows** along a street.
2. To **row** is to pull the oars of a boat to make it move. Carol **rowed** across the lake.

rub

When you move things back and forth, they **rub** together. I am **rubbing** my hands together to make them warm. I **rubbed** the table to make it shine.

rug

A **rug** is a piece of thick cloth that covers the floor.

rule

A **rule** is something that must be obeyed. Games like football have **rules**. In the United States traffic drives on the right. That is the **rule**.

The big wheel at the fair is **round**.

run

If you move fast, kicking out one leg after another, you **run**. I saw a hen **running** down the road. Some animals are very fast **runners**. I **ran** to my room to fetch my book.

Three **runners** are **running** in a race.

How many **sails** does this boat have?

sad
We feel **sad** when we feel unhappy. Meg felt **sad** when she broke her favorite doll.

saddle
When you ride a horse, you sit in the **saddle**. A **saddle** is a leather seat fastened to the horse with straps.

Erica sat **safely** in the **saddle**.

safe
It is not **safe** to play with fire. Things that are **safe** are things that cannot hurt you.

sail
A **sail** is a large piece of cloth on a boat. The wind blows against the **sail** and pushes the boat forward. When we travel in a boat with a **sail**, we are **sailing**. People who go **sailing** are called **sailors**. Have you ever **sailed**?

salt
We put **salt** on our food to make it tasty. The sea is **salty**. **Salt** is made of tiny white crystals.

same
When things are the **same**, they are alike. Matt's hair is the **same** color as a carrot. My birthday is on the **same** day as yours.

sand
The children built a castle in the **sand**. **Sand** is made of tiny pieces of rock. We love to play on a **sandy** beach.

146

sandal

A **sandal** is a kind of open shoe held to the foot with straps. We wear **sandals** in summer to keep our feet cool.

Santa Claus

My Mom says that **Santa Claus** visits good children on Christmas Eve and leaves them a present. She says that **Santa Claus** lives at the North Pole.

Saturday

Saturday is the seventh day of the week. On **Saturdays** we don't have to go to school. "**Saturday's** child works hard for a living," says the old rhyme.

save

1. If you keep your money and don't spend it, you **save** it. Don't eat all the apples – **save** one for Tom.
2. To **save** also means to rescue. The man jumped into the sea and **saved** Bob from drowning.

saw

A **saw** is a tool for cutting hard things like wood and metal. **Saws** have an edge with sharp teeth.

school (skool)

A **school** is a place where you go to learn things. **School** teaches you how to read and write. You also have lots of fun at **school** with your friends.

science

Science is the name given to the things we learn about our world. Biology is a **science**. In biology, we learn about the life of plants.

scissors (sizz-ers)

Scissors are a cutting tool. Two sharp metal blades held together at the middle rub against each other to cut paper and cloth. The hairdresser uses special **scissors** to cut hair.

scratch

Cats **scratch** themselves with their claws. If you have an itch, you must **scratch** it. When you **scratch**, you rub against something with a sharp point.

screen

Your television has a **screen**. The pictures appear on the **screen**.

screw

A **screw** is a piece of metal which holds two pieces of wood together. A nail is smooth, but a **screw** has a curved edge to grip the wood.

sea

The large area of salt water that covers most parts of the earth is called **sea**. We like to swim in the **sea**.

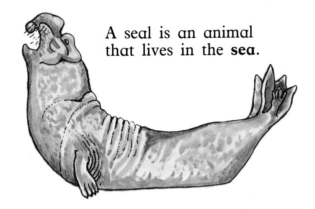

A seal is an animal that lives in the **sea**.

seal

A **seal** is an animal that lives most of the time in or near the sea. Tame **seals** can be taught to do tricks with a ball.

season

A **season** is one fourth of the year. The four **seasons** are spring, summer, autumn (or fall), and winter.

second

There are sixty **seconds** in a minute. A **second** is a very short length of time.

secret

A **secret** is something you don't want anyone to know about. Sometimes you tell a **secret** to a good friend.

see

We **see** with our eyes. Have you **seen** the ghost? Yes, I **saw** it last night with its head held under its arm. You must have been **seeing** things!

seed

Most plants grow from tiny **seeds**. Dave has planted **seeds** in the garden.

sell

The store owner will **sell** you candy if you pay money. The store owner **sells** the things that you buy.

send

Send me a postcard from France. To **send** means to make someone or something go from one place to another. I **sent** John to the store to get some butter.

September

September is the ninth month of the year. Most children start their new school year in **September**.

seven (7)

Seven is a number. There are **seven** days in the week.

sew (so)

To **sew** means to hold cloth together with a needle and thread.

shadow

If something moves in front of the light, it will make a **shadow** on the ground. Watch the shape of your **shadow** on the next sunny day.

shake

Shake means to move something up and down or from side to side. **Shake** the dust out of the mat. I **shook** you to wake you up.

shape

A circle is a round **shape**. Everything you can see has a **shape**. The line round the outside of something makes its **shape**.

share

If you give other people a part of what you have, you **share** it.

sharp

All tools that cut have **sharp** edges. Use a **sharp** knife to cut the cheese.

she

Nan is a girl. **She** is a girl. Give Nan a pear. Give **her** a pear. **Her** name is Nan.

sheep

A **sheep** is an animal. The hair of **sheep** is called wool. We make cloth from wool. I can see ten **sheep** in the field.

shelf

A **shelf** is a long piece of wood or metal fixed to a wall or frame. You put things on **shelves**. I have a row of books on my bedroom **shelves**.

Snails have soft bodies. They live inside **shells**.

shell

Many animals and fish protect themselves in a hard covering called a **shell**. The snail hides in its **shell** when it is frightened. Eggs are protected in **shells**.

shine

Bright things give off light or **shine**. When the sun is **shining**, my bedroom is full of light.

ship

A **ship** is a big boat. Some **ships** carry people across the ocean. I sail a model **ship** in my bath.

shirt

I wore my best **shirt** and pants for the party. A **shirt** is worn on the top part of the body. It has buttons down the front and has a collar.

What **size shoes** do you wear?

shoe

John put his left **shoe** on his right foot! **Shoes** keep your feet warm and dry. Horses have iron **shoes** fitted to their hooves.

shoot

To **shoot** means to use a gun or a bow and arrow. When you **shoot** you try to hit something with a bullet or arrow.

shop

We buy things from a **shop**. Each **shop** sells different things. The baker's **shop** sells bread.

shore

The edge of the sea is called the **shore**. The fishermen pull their boats up onto the **shore** each night.

short

Short people are not tall. A **short** string is not long.

shoulder

Your **shoulder** is where your arm joins the rest of your body. Grandma put a blanket around her **shoulders.**

shout

A **shout** is a loud call. The boy **shouted** across the street to his friend.

show

To **show** means to point out or let somebody see something. Can you **show** me the tallest tower? **Show** your friends the gifts you got for Christmas.

shut

To **shut** is the same as to close. Your eyes **shut** when you go to sleep. They are not open.

sick

When you are **sick**, you do not feel well.

side

Side means a part of something. Often it means the part at the edge. The **sides** of the box stop the apples from falling out. Eddie walks his dog by the **side** of the river.
The two teams in a football game are called **sides**. Which **side** are you playing for?

sign

A **sign** is a big notice. It tells you something. This **sign** says "One Way."

silver

Silver is a shiny, white metal. Spoons and forks are sometimes made of silver. So are the shiny cups that are presented to sports champions.

sing

When we **sing**, we make music with our voices. The birds **sing** when the sun rises. We **sang** songs at summer camp. Have you ever **sung** a song?

single

Single means there is only one. Can I have a **single** bed in this hotel?

sink

1. If you drop a stone into a pool, it will **sink** to the bottom. To **sink** means to drop down. The ship **sank** to the sea bed. The divers found the **sunken** ship.
2. We washed our hands in the **sink**. A **sink** is a washing bowl in the kitchen.

sister

Your **sister** is a girl who has the same mother and father as you have.

sit

When you rest on a chair, you **sit** on it. Are you **sitting** comfortably? The cat **sat** on my lap.

six (6)

Six is the number that follows five. Insects have **six** legs.

size

The **size** of something is how big or small it is. That dress is a smaller **size** than this one.

skeleton

The bones of your body fit together to make a **skeleton**. The scientist found **skeletons** of dinosaurs in the rocks.

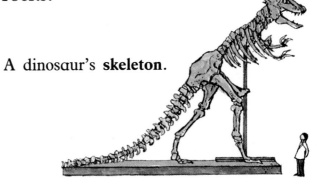

A dinosaur's **skeleton**.

skin

Your body is covered with **skin**. Some animals have very thick **skin**.

skirt

A **skirt** is a piece of clothing that girls and women wear.
Skirts hang from the waist and cover the lower parts of the body.

Angela is wearing a grass **skirt**.

sky

When you look up out of doors the **sky** is above you. Today clouds are covering the sun and the **sky** is gray.

slow

A snail moves at a very **slow** speed. **Slow** is the opposite of fast.

small

Small things are little. They are not big. The mouse is **smaller** than the elephant, but the fly is the **smallest** of all.

smell

We **smell** with our noses. Flowers have a good **smell**, but some animals don't **smell** so good.

smile

A **smile** is a happy look on somebody's face. You lift the corners of your mouth when you smile.

smoke

When things burn, they give off **smoke**. **Smoke** rises in a dark gray cloud.

smooth

Smooth things do not feel rough. Your skin feels **smooth**. A pebble is **smooth**. It has no sharp edges.

snail

A **snail** is an animal that carries a hard shell on its back.

A **snake's** jaw can open so wide that it can eat an egg whole.

snake

A **snake** is a reptile with a long body and no legs. **Snakes** slide along the ground. Some **snakes** have a poisonous bite.

sneeze

"A-choo" is the kind of noise you make when air suddenly blows out of your mouth and nose. People **sneeze** a lot when they have a cold.

The children built a **snowman**.

snow

When it is very cold, rain freezes into small pieces called flakes which fall as **snow**. **Snow** falls in winter. The children built a **snowman**.

soap

Soap is used for washing. We wash our hands with **soap** and water.

sock

You have a big hole in your **sock**. We wear **socks** on our feet to keep them warm.

soft

Something that is **soft** is not hard or rough. Snow is **soft**. Fur is **soft**. Music can sound **soft** when it is not loud.

soldier

A **soldier** is a person who is in the army. Jane and Bill fought a battle with toy **soldiers.**

something

We use the name **something** to describe a thing that we don't know by name. Have you got **something** in your hand? I saw **something** moving in the shadows.

sometimes

If you do something **sometimes**, you don't do it all the time. **Sometimes** I stay up till midnight.

son

A **son** is the male child of a mother and father.

song

You sing a **song**. **Songs** have words and music.

sorry

If you wish something had not happened, you feel **sorry** about it. The boy is **sorry** that he broke your window.

sound

Any noise that you hear is a **sound**. Airplanes make a very loud **sound** when they take off.

soup

Soup is a liquid food. My favorite kind is tomato **soup**.

sour

Lemons have a **sour** taste. **Sour** is the opposite of sweet.

south

South is the opposite way from north. It is on your right when you face the sun early in the morning.

space

A **space** is another name for a hole. Can you fill the **space** in this w rd?

speak

When you **speak** you make words with your mouth. Who is **speaking** in class? I have **spoken** to the teacher about your violin lessons.

special

Something that is not ordinary is **special**. **Special** things are different from others. They are usually better. Thanksgiving Day is a **special** day.

spell

1. When you can **spell**, you know which letters make up each word.
2. Witches know how to make magic **spells**, which is something very different!

spend

1. If you want to buy a new bike, you will have to **spend** your money. How much money have you **spent**?
2. To **spend** time means to pass time doing something. I **spent** my summer vacation in Canada.

spider

A **spider** is a small, buglike animal with eight legs.

spin

1. To **spin** means to turn and turn. A record **spins** on a record player.
2. Bits of cotton and wool are **spun** into strong threads. The spider **spins** thread in its body to make its web.

splash

A **splash** is made when something falls into water. The man **splashed** into the pool.

spoon

A **spoon** has a handle and a round part which holds food. You eat ice cream with a **spoon**.

spot

A **spot** is a small mark or point.

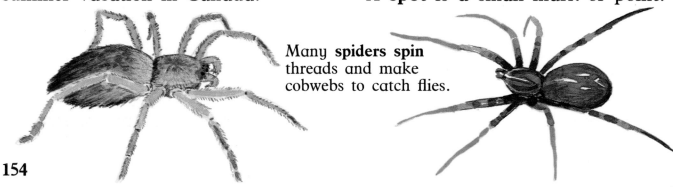

Many **spiders spin** threads and make cobwebs to catch flies.

Spring comes between winter and summer.

spring

1. **Spring** is the season of the year when plants begin to grow and many young birds and animals are born.

2. To **spring** means to jump into the air. The athlete **sprang** over the fence.

square

A shape with four straight sides, all the same length, is called a **square**. This book is not **square**.

squirrel

A **squirrel** is an animal with a big tail. **Squirrels** live in trees and feed mainly on nuts.

stairs

A set of steps to walk up and down is known as **stairs**. The children ran up the **stairs** to the top of the tower.

stand

When we **stand** we are on our feet. We are not sitting. The boy is **standing** on my hat. The children **stood** very still.

star

A **star** is a distant sun that you can see as a tiny bright light in the sky at night. **Stars** are many, many millions of miles away from us.

start

When we **start**, we begin. When I've counted to three, you **start** to sing. Why haven't you **started** your breakfast?

station

A **station** is a stopping place. The train stopped at the **station**. We filled the car at the gas **station**. A **station** is also a building with a special use. We reported the accident to the police **station**.

steal

To **steal** means to take something that is not your own. Jock **stole** my bear. Who has **stolen** my boat?

steam

Water turns to gas when it boils. As it turns to gas, it makes a mist called **steam**.

stem

The thin part of a plant that holds up flowers or leaves is called a **stem**.

step

We take a **step** each time we move a foot backward or forward.

stick

1. **Stick** these sheets of paper together. To **stick** means the same as to glue.
2. A **stick** is a long, thin piece of wood.

sting

A bee or wasp will **sting** to protect itself. The insect's **sting** is in its tail.

stitch

A **stitch** can be made by pulling a needle and thread through cloth. All your clothes are sewn together with **stitches**.

stomach

The **stomach** is a bag in your body where your food collects. The food is mixed and softened in the **stomach**.

stone

Stones are pieces of rock. We use the **stone** to build walls. Some **stones**, like rubies and emeralds, are worth a lot of money. They are called precious **stones** or gemstones.

These **stones** are worth a lot of money. They are precious **stones**.

stop

When you put an end to doing something, you **stop**. The police officer **stopped** the traffic. **Stop** crying and cheer up!

store

Squirrels **store** nuts for the winter. When you **store** something, you keep it in a safe place for some time. **Stores** are the places where you buy food.

storm

When heavy rain falls and there is lightning and thunder, a **storm** is taking place. The wind blows the sea into high waves during a **storm**.

Grandma is reading Sue a **story**.

story

1. An adventure which you read or which someone tells you is a **story**. Dad reads scary ghost **stories** to us every night.
2. A **story** is also a floor of a building. Our building has forty **stories.**

straight

A **straight** line goes from one point to another without bending. You can draw a **straight** line with a ruler.

strange

Something that is **strange** is new or unusual. I saw a **strange** animal in the park. It had green and pink ears!

strap

A **strap** is a kind of belt that is used to close a suitcase or a piece of clothing. Close the **straps** on your luggage or it will open.

strawberry

A **strawberry** is a red, juicy fruit that grows in the summer. I love **strawberries** and cream.

street

A **street** is a road in a town. The shops are on Main **Street**.

stretch

Elastic **stretches** if you pull it. I **stretch** my arms and legs when I get out of bed in the morning. To **stretch** means to pull and make longer.

Pam has just woken up. She is **stretching** her arms.

string

We use **string** to tie up parcels. **String** is a strong thread.

stripe

A **stripe** is a narrow line. The flag of the United States has red and white **stripes.**

strong

Strong people have powerful muscles. They can lift heavy weights. Onions have a **strong** smell.

submarine

A **submarine** is a boat that can move under water. **Submarine** means "under the sea."

subtract

To **subtract** means to take away. What is four **subtracted** from six?

sum

When you add a group of numbers together you find the total or **sum.** What is the **sum** of the bill?

summer

Summer is the warmest season of the year. Let's go to the seashore during our **summer** vacation.

sun

On a fine day, we can see the **sun** in the sky. The **sun** is a ball of burning gases.

A **submarine** is a boat that can travel under water.

sugar

We put **sugar** on our food to make it taste sweet. **Sugar** is sweet.

suit

A group of things that go together is called a **suit.** You wear a **suit** of clothes. Those two naughty children are **suited** to each other.

Sunday

Sunday is the first day of the week.

supermarket

A **supermarket** is a large store. You can help yourself to all kinds of things in a **supermarket,** but be sure to pay at the checkout counter!

surprise

When something happens that you do not expect, it is a **surprise**. John jumped out at Mary and **surprised** her.

swallow

You **swallow** when you let food or drink go down your throat.

swan

A **swan** is a large white bird with a long neck. A baby **swan** is called a cygnet.

The **swan** and her cygnets are **swimming** on the water.

swim

Animals that move in water can **swim**. You **swim** by pushing forward with your arms and legs. Jo is a good **swimmer**. She **swam** out to the rocks.

swing

When you move from side to side, or backward and forward, you **swing**. The monkey is **swinging** from the branch. It **swung** through the trees.

sweep

We use a broom to **sweep** the floor. When we **sweep**, we brush away the dust.

sweet

Sugar is **sweet**. Do you like **sweet** tea? **Sweet** is the opposite of sour.

synagogue

People who belong to the Jewish faith worship in a building called a **synagogue**.

The monkey is hanging by its **tail**.

table
A **table** is a piece of furniture to put things on. It has a flat top. We sit at the **table** to eat.

tail
Animals have a **tail**. It is the end of the backbone that sticks out behind. Dogs wag their **tails** when they're happy.

take
When you hold something in your hands, you **take** it. You may pick it up in one place and **take** it to another. I am **taking** the letters to post them. She **took** the coat out of the cloakroom. Nick has **taken** his radio to school.

talk
When we speak words to each other, we **talk**. We **talked** on the phone last night.

tall
Trees are **tall**. They go up a long way from the ground. Giants are even **taller**.

tame
Animals that are pets are **tame**. Some wild animals can be **tamed**, like monkeys.

taste
The food we eat **tastes** good. Sugar has a sweet **taste**. Lemons have a sour **taste**. We **taste** food with our tongue.

taxicab

He called for a **taxicab** to go to the airport. You pay to travel in automobiles called **taxicabs**.

tea

The leaves of the **tea** plant are dried and pressed into bits. We mix these with boiling water to make a drink called **tea**.

These Indian women are picking leaves of the **tea** plant. Do you like the **taste** of **tea**?

teach

At school, **teachers teach** children how to do many things. Our **teacher taught** us how to speak Spanish today.

team

A number of people play a game together as a **team**. The **teams** met to play a game of hockey.

tear (rhymes with hair)

When you **tear** a piece of paper, you rip or break it. Jane **tore** her jeans on a nail.

tear (rhymes with fear)

A **tear** is a drop of water that runs from your eye when you cry. Wipe your **tears** with this tissue.

tease

Tease means to make fun of someone. Mike laughed at his brother when he fell off his bike. He **teased** him.

telephone (tell-a-fone)

You can talk to someone who is far away by using the **telephone**. The sound of your voice is carried by electricity from one **telephone** to another. Answer the **phone** when it rings.

The **teams** met to play a game of hockey.

television

We see moving pictures on the screen of a **television**. There are many kinds of programs on TV. Do you like watching movies on **television?**

tell

When we **tell** each other something, we talk together. Mommy **tells** us a story each night. The man **told** us that the circus was coming.

temperature

The **temperature** tells us how hot or cold something is. The **temperature** outside is freezing. She had a high **temperature** when she was ill.

ten (10)

Ten is a number. We have **ten** fingers.

tennis

Tennis is a game played with a racket and a ball. **Tennis** players hit the ball to each other over a net.

You play **tennis** with a **tennis** ball and a **tennis** racket.

tent

A **tent** is a shelter made of material that can be folded up and carried with you. The scouts put up their **tents** in the farmer's field.

Many people in deserts live in **tents**. They move from place to place to look for food and water.

test

When you **test** something, you try it out. My Mom **tested** the light to see if it worked. You can also **test** people to find out how much they know about something.

thanksgiving

Thanksgiving is a holiday that we celebrate in our country each November. On **Thanksgiving** day we give thanks for all we have.

the

The is a useful word. It is used to talk about one particular thing. **The** cat was stuck in **the** tree.

theater

A **theater** is a place where you can see a play or a motion picture.

162

then

Then tells us when something happened. Yesterday we played in the sand, **then** we went swimming.

there

There tells us where something is or happened. The sea is over **there**. **There** is a boat near the cliff.

thermometer

We use a **thermometer** to help us find out the temperature. The doctor put a **thermometer** in the sick boy's mouth.

thick

A **thick** coat keeps us warm. Animals with **thick** coats have a heavy covering of hair. A **thick** wall is a wide wall.

thin

Thin is the opposite of thick. A sheet of paper is **thin**.

think

When people **think,** they are using their brains. I am **thinking** how to work out this problem. Yesterday I **thought** about my sister.

thirsty

When you want a drink, you feel **thirsty.** Playing games can make you **thirsty**.

thousand

A **thousand** is one hundred ten times. A **thousand** is also written like this: 1,000.

The **temperature** in cold lands is freezing. Bears **there** have **thick** coats.

thread

A **thread** is a thin, long piece of material used for sewing.

three (3)

Three is a small number. A cycle with **three** wheels is called a tricycle.

throat

You swallow food down your **throat**. You also cough to clear your **throat**.

through (throo)

When you pass **through** a doorway, you move from one room to another **through** a hole in the wall. The circus dog jumped **through** the hoop.

throw

To **throw** means to toss. **Throw** me the ball. I **threw** a stone at the window. The potatoes were **thrown** into a sack.

The subway train is coming **through** the tunnel. Have you bought a **ticket** for the ride?

thumb

Your **thumb** is the short, fat finger on the inside of your hand. Babies sometimes suck their **thumbs**.

thump

A **thump** is a heavy, dull sound.

thunder

Thunder is a loud rumbling noise in the sky. We often hear **thunder** during a storm.

Thursday

Thursday is the fifth day of the week. "**Thursday's** child has far to go," says the old rhyme.

ticket

A **ticket** is a small piece of paper that tells how much you paid for something. Buy a **ticket** for the ball game.

tidy

Tidy means neat, clean and in order. Jan keeps her bedroom very **tidy**. Everything is in its place.

tie

When we **tie** something up, we make sure it won't move from a certain place. **Tie** your shoelace, or your shoe will come off. The sailor **tied** a knot in the rope.

Tigers are the biggest members of the cat family. They are very strong.

tiger
A **tiger** is a large wild animal of the cat family. It has a black and yellow striped fur.

time
The **time** tells us what hour it is. It is **time** to go to bed. I had a good **time** at the zoo.

tiny
Tiny things are very small. A mouse is a **tiny** animal. A flea is **tiny**, too!

tire
A **tire** is a rubber cover put on a wheel. It is filled with air. It helps a wheel roll along more smoothly.

tired
When you feel sleepy, you are **tired**. Bobby felt very **tired** after he won the race. I'm **tired** of doing homework. Sometimes you get **tired** of things that go on for a long time.

tissue
Tissue is a soft paper. We use **tissue** handkerchiefs.

What **time** is it? Please tell me the **time**. I am **tired**. It is my bed**time**.

today
Today is this day. If tomorrow is Tuesday, what day is **today**?

toe
You have five **toes** at the end of each foot.

together
Things that are close are **together**. Friends like to stay close and do things **together**. The two boys played **together** in the tree house.

tomato

A **tomato** is a fruit that is usually red. We eat **tomatoes** in a salad.

tomorrow

Tomorrow will come after today. If today is Saturday what day will it be **tomorrow**?

tongue

Your **tongue** is the part of your mouth that helps you talk and taste. Cats drink milk with their **tongues**. Toads catch insects with their **tongues**.

tonight

Tonight is the end of today. I want to stay up late **tonight**.

ton

A **ton** is a measure of weight. A **ton** is a very heavy weight to lift.

tool

A **tool** helps us work. Hammers and screwdrivers are **tools** we use in the house.

tooth

A **tooth** is a hard part in your mouth. You need your **teeth** to bite and chew food.

top

The highest part of anything is the **top**. The roof is the **top** part of a house. I wonder what you can see from the **top** of the Eiffel Tower, in Paris.

tortoise

A **tortoise** is an animal with a thick hard shell on its back. **Tortoises** move very slowly.

touch

To **touch** means to put your hand on something and feel it. Close your eyes and **touch** your nose.

towel

There is a **towel** in the bathroom to dry yourself with. Towels are made of cloth.

Car

Truck

Trailer

Van

The Eiffel **Tower** has platforms from which people can look over Paris. They can watch the **traffic** on the roads below. Would you like to go to the **top** of the **tower**?

tower

A **tower** is a tall building or part of a building. The Eiffel **Tower** is famous. It is in Paris, France.

town

A **town** is a large place where people work and live. A **town** is smaller than a city.

toy

Do you have a favorite **toy**? **Toys** are things that children play with. Dolls and kites are **toys**.

track

A **track** is a set of rails on which a train moves.

tractor

A farmer drives a **tractor** in the fields. A **tractor** is a vehicle used for pulling carts and plows. It has large wheels to help it move through the mud.

traffic

All the cars and trucks that move on the road are called **traffic**. Too many cars on the road will cause a **traffic** jam.

Cars and buses and motorbikes and trucks and vans are all traveling along the highway. There is a lot of **traffic**.

Bus

Car transporter

Motorcycle

Sports car

train

A **train** is a long line of railroad cars. **Trains** are pulled along a track by an engine.

travel

When we move from one place to another, we **travel**. They **traveled** around the world in a small boat. My aunt is a great **traveler**. She likes seeing new places.

treasure

We found an old map that showed where the **treasure** was buried. Such things as money and jewels are known as **treasures**.

tree

A **tree** is a tall plant with branches and leaves. Lots of **trees** together are called a forest. We get wood from trees.

Trees are the biggest of all plants. The main part of a **tree** is its trunk. Branches grow from the trunk. Leaves grow on the branches. The roots of a **tree** are below the ground.

triangle

A **triangle** is a shape with three straight sides.

The sides of these pyramids in Egypt are in the shape of a **triangle**. **Triangles** have three sides.

Turtles and tortoises live in shells.
Turtles spend most of their time in the sea.

trick

Do you ever play a **trick** on your friends? A **trick** is a joke or a clever puzzle.

truck

A **truck** is a vehicle. It carries heavy loads from place to place.

true

If something is true, it is real. When you tell the **truth**, you say what really happened. Is it **true** that dinosaurs once lived?

trumpet

A **trumpet** is a long metal instrument which is blown into to make musical sounds.

try

I **try** to catch the ball. You find out if you can do something by **trying**. I am **trying** to learn my multiplication table. The man **tried** to lift the weights.

Tuesday

Tuesday is the day after Monday. "**Tuesday's** child is full of grace," says the old rhyme.

tunnel

A **tunnel** is a hole through a hill or underground. A mole **tunnels** through the earth.

turn

To **turn** is to go around. The wheels **turn** to make the bicycle move along.

turtle

A **turtle** is very like a tortoise. **Turtles** have hard shells and live in the sea.

twice

I have bathed **twice** today. I bathed once this morning and once this evening. That makes two times.

twin

One thing that is like another is its **twin**. Those **twin** sisters look the same.

two (2)

Two is a number. **Two** things that go together are called a pair.

typewriter

We use a **typewriter** to print letters. It is a kind of printing machine.

Uu

ugly

Ugly things are not pretty to look at. The **ugly** toad changed into a handsome prince.

I may look **ugly** but I am really very nice!

In the rain I keep dry **under** my **umbrella**.

umbrella

An **umbrella** is something you hold over your head to keep off the rain. It is made of a frame covered with material.

uncle

My father's brother is my **uncle**. So is my mother's brother. My **uncle** is married to my aunt.

under

To be below or beneath something is to be **under** it. The water flows **under** the bridge.

understand

Do you **understand** what you are reading? Do you know what the words mean? To **understand** means to know about the thing you are doing, or the words you are hearing. I **understood** what she said in French.

unhappy

To be **unhappy** is to feel sad. Janice cried because she was so **unhappy**.

uniform

Soldiers wear **uniforms**; so do police officers. A **uniform** is a special suit of clothing.

United States

One part of North America is formed into one country. It is known as the **United States** of America.

untidy

When things are scattered around in a messy way, they look **untidy**. My hair is **untidy**, so I will tie it back with a ribbon.

My sister is very **untidy**. She leaves her things everywhere. She is messy.

up

To go **up** means to rise. I went **up** the hill. I flew my kite **up** in the air.

I can see you **upside down**.

upside down

When something is **upside down** it means that the top is where the bottom should be. If you do a headstand, your body is **upside down.**

upstairs

The top floors of a building are the **upstairs** parts. Our kitchen is downstairs, but my bedroom is **upstairs**. John went **upstairs** to bed.

use

We **use** a cup to drink out of. A broken cup is of no **use**. Things we can **use** are **useful**. Broken tools are **useless**.

usually

Jane **usually** has an egg for breakfast. If something **usually** happens, it happens most of the time.

171

vacation
You enjoy a **vacation** when you take a holiday. We went to Spain on **vacation.**

vanish
Vanish is another word for disappear.

vegetable
A plant that we cook and eat is called a **vegetable**. A potato is a **vegetable**, and so is a leafy cabbage.

vehicle
A **vehicle** is a machine that carries people or things. Cars, trucks, and trains are all **vehicles**.

very
The sun was **very** hot. It was hotter than usual. Ice is **very** cold. It is especially cold to touch.

view
If you look out of the window of a tall building, you will have a good **view** of the land around. They had a **view** of the sea from the hotel window.

violin
The **violin** is a musical instrument. A stick called a bow is pulled across four tight strings to make different sounds. People who play **violins** are known as **violinists**.

visit
When you **visit** someone, you go to see them. The boy **visited** his friend. How many **visitors** are you expecting today?

voice
Your **voice** is the sound you make when you speak or sing. The singer has a wonderful **voice**. John shouted in a loud **voice**.

volcano
When the hot liquid inside the earth pushes its way to the earth's surface, it explodes in a **volcano**.

vulture
A **vulture** is a large bird that feeds off the remains of dead animals. It is part of the group of birds we call birds of prey.

The Great **Wall** of China.

wagon

A **wagon** is a four-wheeled cart used for carrying heavy loads. The **wagon** was piled high with fruit.

waist

The part of your body between your chest and your stomach is called your **waist**. Tim is wearing a belt around his **waist**.

wait

I am **waiting** for my friend to come. I am expecting him to come. We all stood at the bus stop and **waited** for the bus to come.

wake

Wake means to stop sleeping. Our dog **woke** up early this morning.

walk

When we put one foot in front of another to move along the ground, we are **walking**. Take the dogs for a **walk**. We **walked** all the way to town through the deep snow.

wall

A **wall** can be built of bricks or stones. A room usually has four **walls**. The Chinese built a high **wall** along the boundary of their country. It is over three thousand miles long. It is called the Great **Wall** of China.

want

To **want** is to need or wish for something you haven't got. Joe **wants** a puppy. He has **wanted** one for a long time.

The puppy **wants** to come home with me.

war

A **war** happens when two countries fight each other. Many soldiers were killed in the Second World **War**.

warm

When you feel **warm** you feel a little hot. I'd rather be warm than cold. The sun makes us feel **warm**.

I am **washing** in **warm water**.

wash

We **wash** our hands in water to get them clean. It is best to use soap when you **wash**. Have you **washed** behind your ears?

waste

The word **waste** means something that can't be used. We **waste** food when we cannot eat it. Don't **waste** time doing nothing!

watch

1. To **watch** means to look at for a time. I would like to **watch** television this afternoon.

2. We wear a **watch** to tell the time. The figures on some **watches** glow in the dark.

water

Water is a liquid. It falls from the sky as rain. It fills rivers, lakes and the oceans. We drink **water** and also wash in it.

wave

1. The wind blows across the surface of the sea and makes **waves**. The **waves** are crashing against the rocks.
2. When we **wave**, we move our arms. The children **waved** at their father.

We are **watching** the parade and **waving** our flags.

weak

Weak things are not strong. Most baby animals and plants are **weak** until they begin to grow stronger.

wear

When we put on clothes, we **wear** them. My aunt is **wearing** an unusual hat. Has she **worn** it before? Clothes that are used too much will **wear** out. The elbows on your old sweater are very **worn**. I **wore** my jeans yesterday.

weather

When it rains or snows, we say the **weather** is bad. When the sun shines, we have good **weather**.

Wednesday

Wednesday is the fourth day of the week. "**Wednesday's** child is full of woe," says the old rhyme.

Whales live in the sea. They are always **wet**! They **weigh** more than any other animal in the world.

week

A **week** has seven days. Sunday is the first day of the **week**. There are fifty-two **weeks** in a year.

weigh

You **weigh** things to see how heavy they are. The man in the shop **weighed** the potatoes we bought. Can you guess my **weight**?

well

1. A **well** is a deep hole that is dug in the ground. They dig a **well** through rock to find oil or water.
2. **Well** also means feeling good. After you have been sick you start to get **well** again. How **well** did you do in your exams?

west

West is the direction that is opposite to east. The sun sets in the **west** each evening.

wet

Water is **wet**. Things that are **wet** are not dry. Jake stood in the rain and got **wet**.

whale

The **whale** is the biggest animal there is. Whales live in the sea. When it is born, a baby blue **whale** is bigger than a grown elephant!

175

what

What asks a question when you want to find out some information. **What** do you want? **What** are you doing?

wheat

Wheat is a grass that is grown by farmers. The **wheat** seeds are crushed into flour to make bread.

wheel

A **wheel** is a round shape that turns on its center. **Wheels** help trucks and trains move.

when

When asks a question. It asks about the time that something happened. **When** did you break the window with your football? **When** also tells you the time that something happens. I will be happy **when** my brother comes home.

where

Where asks a question or tells you about a place. **Where** did the bird build its nest? The scissors are **where** I left them.

which

Which asks a question about two or more things or people. **Which** bottle holds the most water? **Which** boy is the tallest?

whisper

To **whisper** is to speak very softly. You **whisper** when you don't want everyone to hear what you are saying.

whistle

Blow softly through your lips to make a **whistle** noise. The man **whistled** to his dog. The referee blew his **whistle** to finish the game.

The tractor and combine harvester in this **wheat** field move along on **wheels**.

white

Things that have no color are **white**. Snow is **white**.

who

Who asks a question about a person. **Who** are you?

whole

The boy ate the **whole** pie. He ate all of it, not just a part. I read the **whole** book in two hours.

why

Why asks a question. We use it when we want to know the reason that something happened. **Why** did the chicken cross the road? **Why** are you looking at me?

wide

The space from one side to another tells you how **wide** it is. How **wide** is the Atlantic Ocean? I want you to stand with your legs **wide** apart. The distance across is called the **width**.

wife

When a woman marries a man she becomes his **wife**.

wild

Wild animals do not usually live near people. They find their own food. Lions are **wild** animals when they live in Africa. Lions that live in zoos are also **wild**. They are tame when they have been taught to live as people want. **Wild** means untamed. Plants that do not grow in our gardens are **wild** plants.

win

When you **win**, you do better than other people in a race or competition. That horse is **winning** the race. Has it **won** the cup?

wind

When air moves it makes a **wind**. A strong **wind** is called a gale or hurricane. The clouds are blown along by the **wind**.

wind (rhymes with kind)

To **wind** means to turn round. A key **winds** up a clock. String is **wound** into a ball. Grandma is **winding** a ball of yarn.

window

A **window** is an opening in a wall that is filled in with glass. The sunlight comes in through the **window**. Open the **window** and let in the fresh air.

wing

A **wing** is a kind of arm. Birds, insects and airplanes have **wings** to help them fly.

Hedgehogs are **wild** animals.

winter

Winter is the name of the coldest season of the year. In **winter** the days are short and cold.

wipe

When I have washed up I will **wipe** the dishes. To **wipe** means to dry or clean with a cloth.

wire

A **wire** is a long thin piece of metal. Electricity passes along **wires** in your house.

wish

We **wish** for things we haven't got. He **wished** he had a cat. The princess had three **wishes**.

witch

In fairy stories, a **witch** is usually a bad woman. **Witches** are said to ride on broomsticks and make magic spells.

Witches are **women** who are said to make magic spells.

with

When two things are **with** each other, they are together. Jake went **with** his sister to the toy shop. He went **without** his money. **Without** is the opposite of **with**. You don't have something if you are **without** it.

wizard

A **wizard** is a magic man. Merlin was a famous **wizard** who gave his king a magic sword.

Wolves live mostly in **woods** in cold parts of the **world**.

wolf

A **wolf** is a wild animal that looks like a dog. **Wolves** hunt in packs and are very fierce.

woman

A **woman** is a grown up female person. The **women** went to the store to buy eggs.

won See **win**.

wood

Wood comes from trees. A group of trees is sometimes called the **woods**. **Wood** can be cut up and made into furniture.

wool

A sheep's coat is made of **wool**. This coat is cut off once a year and made into a fine thread. Jane's sweater is made from **wool**.

word

Letters can be joined together to form **words**. The letters "c," "a," and "t" can be used to make the **word** "cat." This dictionary is full of words.

work

When we do a job, we **work** to finish a task. My mom **works** in a bank. Let's finish our **homework** and then we can go out to play.

world

The planet we live on is sometimes called the **world**. Yachts are sailed around the **world**.

worm

A **worm** is a long, thin animal without legs. It tunnels underground. Birds eat **worms**.

There are hundreds of different kinds of **worms**.

wrap

We **wrap** up in warm clothes when it is cold. We **wrap** up things when we cover them in material or paper. John **wrapped** up Jane's birthday present in red paper.

In **winter** we **wrap** up in warm clothes.

wrist (rist)

The **wrist** is part of your arm above your hand that bends. Do you wear a watch on your **wrist**?

write

I am going to **write** a story. When we use a pen or pencil to make words on paper we are **writing**. Have you **written** to your aunt? Yes, I **wrote** yesterday.

wrong

We do **wrong** when we do something we shouldn't. John got his answers **wrong**. She told me the moon is made of cheese, but I think she's **wrong**.

X ray

An **X ray** is a special kind of light wave. Cameras using **X rays** take pictures of the bones in your body. At the hospital, the doctor took an **X ray** of my broken arm.

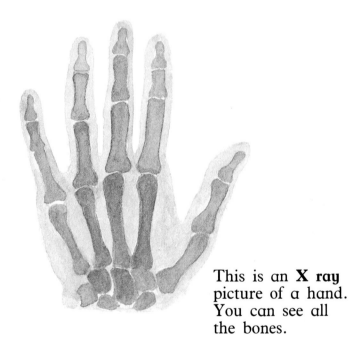

This is an **X ray** picture of a hand. You can see all the bones.

xylophone (zy-le-fone)

A **xylophone** is a musical instrument made of pieces of metal or wood. When you hit the pipes, they make a sound.

A **yacht** is a small boat with sails.

yacht

A **yacht** is a boat with sails. John has a model **yacht**.

yard

1. A **yard** is a measurement. It is the same length as thirty-six inches or three feet.
2. A **yard** is the area that surrounds a house. We wish we had a swimming pool in our backyard.

year

A **year** lasts 365 days. Mary has a birthday once a **year**.

yellow

Yellow is a color. The zipper on this page is colored **yellow**.

180

yes

Yes answers a question. If you say **yes**, you are agreeing with the answer. If you don't agree, you say no.

yesterday

Yesterday is the day before today. **Yesterday** I went to the circus. Tomorrow, today will be **yesterday**!

yolk

The **yolk** is the yellow part of an egg. I like eating eggs when the **yolk** is soft, not hard.

young

You are **young** now, but your grandparents may be old. **Young** people are children. When animals look after their **young**, they care for their babies.

A **zipper** has metal teeth that grip together.

zebra

A **zebra** is a kind of wild horse. It has a black and white striped coat. You can see **zebras** at the zoo.

zero (0)

Zero is another name for none. In winter, there are some places that have a temperature below **zero**. That's cold!

zigzag

A **zigzag** is a line that is broken by sharp corners. Tom rode his skateboard down the street in a **zigzag**.

zipper

Many jackets and pants are fastened with a **zipper**. A **zipper** is made of metal teeth that grip together.

zoo

We see lots of wild animals at the **zoo**. The best kind of **zoo** is one with open pits and grassy areas, where the animals have plenty of space and light.

The Speller Checklist

If you want to be sure how to spell a word, check it on this alphabetical list. Words with an asterisk after them, like this, accelerate★, *are* **not** *in the main part of the dictionary. Words printed in* **heavy black type** *are those which are usually the most difficult to spell.*

A
abacus
abandon★
abbey★
able★
aboard★
aborigines★
about
above
abroad★
absent
absorb★
accelerate★
accept
accident
accommodate★
accurate★
ache
acid★
acorn
acrobat
across
act
acquaint★
actor
actress
add
address
admire
adult
advance
adventure
advertise
advertisement
aerial
affect★
afford
afraid
after
afternoon
afterward★
again

against★
age
ago
agree
ahead
aid★
aim
air
aircraft★
airline★
airplane
airport
alarm
album
alike
alive
all
alligator
allow
alloy★
almost
alone★
along
aloud
alphabet
already
also
alter★
although★
altitude★
altogether
aluminum★
always
amaze
ambulance
ammunition★
among★
amount
amphibian★
an
ancestor★
anchor

ancient★
and
angel
anger★
angle★
angry
animal
ankle
anniversary★
annoy
annual★
another
answer
ant
antelope★
antenna★
antibiotic★
antique★
antler★
any
anyhow★
anyone
anything
anywhere★
apart
ape
apologize
appear
appetite
apple
appointment★
April
apron
aquarium★
aqueduct★
arch
archer★
archery★
architect
Arctic★
area
arena

argument
arithmetic★
arm
armor
army
around
arrange
arrest
arrive
arrow
art★
artificial★
artist
as
ash
ashamed
ask
asleep
aspirin★
astronaut
astronomy★
at
athlete
atlas
atmosphere
atom★
attach★
attack
attempt★
attend★
attract★
audience★
August
aunt
author★
autograph★
automatic★
autumn
avalanche★
avenue
average★
awake

away
ax
axle★

B
baboon
baby
bachelor★
back
backbone★
backward
bacon
bad
badge
badger★
bag
bait★
bake
baker
balance
bald
ball
ballerina★
ballet
balloon
banana
band
bandage
bandit★
bang
bank
bar
barber★
bare★
barge★
bark
barn
barometer★
barrel
base
baseball
basket

basketball
bat
batch★
bath
bathe★
battery★
battle★
bay★
beach
bead★
beak
bean
bear
beard
beast★
beat
beautiful
beaver
became
because
become
bed
bedroom★
bee
beef
beetle
before
beggar★
begin
beginning
behave
behind
believe
bell
belong
below
belt
bench★
bend
beneath★
berry
beside

besides★
best
better★
between
beyond★
Bible
bicycle
big
bill
billion★
binary★
binoculars★
biography★
biology★
biplane★
bird
birth
birthday
biscuit★
bison★
bit★
bite
bitter★
black
blackboard★
blade
blame★
blanket
blaze★
bleed
bless★
blind★
blizzard★
block★
blood★
blossom★
blow
blue
blunder★
blunt
blush★
board

boast★
boat
body
boil
bold★
bolt★
bomb
bone
book
boomerang
boot
border★
borrow
both
bottle
bottom
bought★
bounce
boundary★
bow
bowl
box
boxer★
boy
bracelet★
braille★
brain
brake★
branch
brass★
brave
bread
break
breakfast
breath
breathe★
breeze★
brick
bride★
bridegroom★
bridge
bridle★

bright
brilliant*
brim*
bring
broad*
broke*
broken*
bronze*
brooch*
broom
brother
brought
brown
bruise
brush
bubble
bucket
buckle*
bud
buffalo*
bug
build
building
bulb
bull
bulldozer
bullet
bump
bun*
bunch
bundle
bungalow*
bunk*
buoy*
burglar*
burn
burrow*
burst
bury

bus
bush
business*
busy
butcher*
butter
butterfly
button
buy
by

C
cab
cabbage
cabin*
cactus
café
cage
cake
calculator
calendar
calf
call
calm*
camel
camera
camouflage*
camp
can
canal
candy
cane*
cannon*
canoe

canter*
canvas*
canvass*
cap
cape*
capital
captain
capture
car
card
cardboard
care*
career*
careful*
careless*
cargo*
carnival
carpenter
carpet
carriage
carrot*
carry
cart*
cartoon
carve*
case
cash
cassette*
castanets*
castle
cat
catamaran*
catapult*
catch

caterpillar
cathedral*
cattle
caught*
cause*
cave
cease*
ceiling
cell
cellar
cello*
cement*
cemetery*
census*
cent
centigrade*
centimeter*
centipede
center
century
cereal
ceremony*
certain
certificate*
chain
chair
chalk*
champion
chance*
change
channel*
chapel*
chapter*
character*

charge*
chariot*
charity*
charm*
chase
chatter
cheap
cheat*
check
cheek
cheer*
cheese
chemical*
cherry
chess*
chest
chew*
chicken
chief*
child
children
chimney
chimpanzee
chin
china
chip*
chocolate
choice*
choir*
choke*
choose
chop*
chorus*
chose*
Christian*
Christmas
church
cinema*
circle
circumference*
circus
city
civilization*
civilized*
claim*
clap
clarinet*
class
classroom
claw
clay*
clean
clear
clever

cliff
climate*
climb
clinic*
clock
close
closed
cloth
clothes
cloud
clown
club
clue*
clumsy
coach
coal
coarse*
coast
coat
cobweb
cocoa*
coconut
coffee
coin
cold
collar
collect
college*
collide*
colony*
color
colossal*
column*
comb
combine*
come
comedy*
comet*
comfortable
comic
coming*
comma*
command*
committee*
common*
communicate*
community*
commuter*
company*
compare*
compass
compete*
complain*
complete*

compose*
composer*
computer
concert
concrete*
condense*
conductor*
congratulate*
conifer*
conjurer
connect*
conquer*
conserve*
consider*
consonant*
constellation*
construct*
contain*
container*
contents*
continent*
continue*
control*
convict*
cook
cool*
copper*
copy
coral*
core*
corn*
corner
coronation*
corridor*
cosmonaut*
cost
costume
cottage*
cotton
cough
count
counter*
country
county*
couple
courage*
course*
court*
cousin
cover
cow
coward*
cowboy

crab
crack
cracker
cradle*
craft*
crane
crate*
crater*
crawl
crayon*
cream
create*
creature
creep*
crescent*
crew*
cried*
crime*
criminal*
crimson*
cripple*
crisp*
crocodile
crooked
crop*
cross
crow*
crowd
crown*
cruel
crumb
crush
crust*
cry
crystal
cube
cucumber*
cultivate*
cunning*
cup
cure
curious*
curly*
curry*
curtain*
curve
cushion
custom
customer*
cut
cycle
cygnet*
cylinder*
cymbals*

183

Speller

D
daffodil
dagger
daily*
dairy*
daisy*
dam
damage*
damp
dance*
danger
dare*
dark
dart
date
daughter
day
dead
deaf
dear*
death*
debate*
debt*
decade*
decay*
deceive*
December
decide
decimal*
decision*
deck
declare*
decorate*
decrease*
deed*
deep
deer
defeat*
defend*
delay*
delicate*
delicious
delight*
deliver*
delta*
demand*
democracy*
den
dense*
dentist
deny*
depart*
describe*
desert

deserve*
design*
desire*
desk
dessert*
destroy*
detail*
detective
detergent*
develop*
diagonal*
dial*
diameter*
diamond
diary*
dice
dictionary
die
different
difficult
dig
digestion*
dim*
dinghy*
dinner
dinosaur
dip*
direction*
dirty
disappear
disaster*
discover
discuss
disease*
disguise
dish
dismiss*
display*
distance
distant*
district*
disturb
ditch
dive
diver*
divide
do
dock*
doctor
doesn't*
dog
doll
dollar
dolphin*

dome*
donkey
door
dot
double
doubt*
dough*
down
downstairs
dozen
drag
dragon
drain
drake*
draw
drawer
dream
dress
drill
drink
drip
drive
driver*
drop*
drown
drug*
drum
dry
duck
dull
dumb*
during
dust
duty*
dwarf
dwell*
dye*
dynamite*

E
each
eagle
ear
early
earn*
earning
earring*
earth
earthquake*
easel*
east
Easter
easy
eat

echo
eclipse*
edge
educate*
eel*
effort*
egg
eighth*
either
elastic
elbow
election*
electricity
electronics*
element*
elephant
elf
else*
elsewhere*
embarrass*
embroidery*
emblem*
emerald*
emergency*
emperor*
empire*
employ*
empty
encourage*
encyclopedia*
end
enemy
energy*
engine
enjoy
enormous
enough
enter
entertain*
entrance*
envelope
environment*
envy*
equal
Equator*
equipment*
erase*
errand*
error*
erupt
escalator
escape
eskimo
especially*

estuary*
evaporate*
even
evening
event
ever
every
everybody
everyone*
everything
everywhere
evil
exam*
example*
excellent
except*
excuse
exciting*
exercise
exist*
exit
expect
expedition*
expensive
experiment*
explain
explode
explore
express*
extinct*
extra
extraordinary*
eye
eyebrow
eyelash
eyelid
eyesight

F
fable*
fabric*
face
fact
factory
fade*
fail*
faint*
fair
fairy
falcon*
fall
false
family
famine*

famous
fan*
fang*
far
farm
farmer
fashion*
fast
farther*
farthest*
fasten*
fastener*
fat
father
fault
favorite
fear*
feast*
feather
feature*
February
feed
feel
feet
fell*
female
fence
ferret*
ferry*
fertile*
festival*
fetch
fever*
few
fiction*
field
fierce
fight
figure
fill
film
fin
final*
find
fine
finger
fingerprint*
finish
fir
fire
fire engine
firefighter*
fireworks*
firm*

first
fish
fist
fit
five
fix*
flag
flake
flame
flap
flash*
flat
flatter*
flavor
flea*
flee*
fleece*
fleet*
flesh*
flight*
flipper*
float
flock*
flood*
floor
flour
flow*
flower
flute*
fly
foal
foam*
focused*
fog
fold
follow
food
foot
football
footprint
for*
force*
forehead
foreign*
foreigner*
forest
forget
forgive*
fork
fortnight*
fortune
forward
fossil*
fostermother*

fountain
fox*
fraction*
fragment*
frame*
free
freedom*
freeze
freight*
fresh
friction*
Friday
friend
frighten
frog
from*
front
frost
frown
fruit
fry
fuel*
full
fun
fungus*
funnel*
funny*
fur
furniture
furry*
future

G
gain*
galaxy*
gale*
galleon*
gallery
gallon
gallop
game
gang*
gangster*
gangway*
gap
garage
garden
gas
gasoline
gate
gauge*
gaze*
gear*
geese*

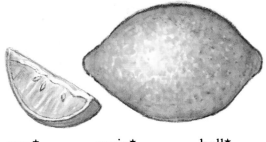

gem*
general*
generator*
generous*
gentle
geography
geology*
geometry*
germ*
get
ghost
giant
gift*
gigantic*
giggle*
gipsy*
giraffe
girl
give
glacier*
glad
glass
glasses*
glide*
glider*
glitter*
globe*
glossary*
glove
glue
gnaw*
gnome
go
goal
goat
god
goddess*
gold
goldfish*
good
goose
gorilla
government
grab
graceful*
gradual*

grain*
grammar*
grandfather*
grandmother*
grandparent
grape*
grasshopper
gravity*
gravy*
gray
graze*
grease*
great
greedy
green
grin*
grind*
grip*
groan*
grocer
groom*
ground
group
grow
growl
grumble*
grunt
guard
guerrilla*
guess
guest*
guide*
guilty
guitar
gulf*
gull*
gum
gun
gunpowder*
gym

H
habit*
hail*
hair
half

hall*
Halloween
halt*
ham*
hamburger
hammer
hamster
hand*
handcuffs*
handicap*
handkerchief*
handle
hang
happen
happy
harbor*
hard
hare*
harm*
harness*
harvest
haste*
hat
hatch*
hate
haul*
haunt*
have
hawk*
hay*
he
head
headquarters*
heal*
health*
healthy*
heap*
hear
heart
heat
heaven
heavy
hedge*
hedgehog*
heel
height*

helicopter
hello
helmet
help
hemisphere*
hen
herb*
herd*
here
hero*
heroine*
hesitate*
hibernate
hiccup*
hide
high
highway*
hijack*
hill
hinge*
hint*
hip*
hippopotamus
history
hit
hobby*
hockey*
hold
hole
hollow
home
honest
honey
hoof
hook
hop
hope
hopeful*
hopeless*
hoping
horizon*
horn
horse
hose
hospital
hot
hotel
hour
house
household*
housekeeper*
hover*
hovercraft*
howl

hug*
hum*
human
humor*
hump
hundred
hunger*
hungry
hunt
hunter*
hurricane*
hurry
hurt
husband
hutch*
hydrofoil*
hydrogen*
hymn*

I
ice
iceberg
icecream
icicle*
icing*
idea
ideal*
if
igloo
ill
illustrate*
illustration*
imitate*
immediately*
impatient*
important
impossible*
improve*
include
increase*
index*
Indian
indoors*
influenza*
information*
inhabit*
inhabitant*
injure*
ink
insect
inside
inspect*
instant*

instantly*
instrument*
interested*
interesting*
interrupt*
introduce*
introduction*
invade*
invent*
invention*
inventor*
invisible
invitation*
invite
iron
island
isn't*
itch*
ivory*

J
jacket
jail*
jam*
January
jar*
jaw*
jealous
jeans*
jelly*
jersey*
jet
jewel
jeweler*
jewelry*
job*
jockey*
jog*
join
joint
joke
jolly*
journalist*
journey*
joy*
judge*
juggler*
juice
July
jump
June
jungle
junior*

K
kaleidoscope*
kangaroo
kayak*
keen*
keep
kennel
kerosene*
ketchup*
kettle*
key
kick
kid
kidnap*
kidney*
kill
kilogram*
kilometer*
kilt*
kind
king
kingdom*
kiss*
kitchen
kite
kitten
kiwi*
knee
kneel
knife
knight*
knit*
knitting*
knob*
knock
knot
know
knowledge*
knuckle*
koala*
kosher*

L
label*
laboratory*
lad*
ladder
lagoon*
lake
lamb
lame*
lamp*
land
landscape*

language
large
larva*
lasso
last
late
laugh
laughter*
launch
law
lawn*
lay
layer*
lazy
lead
leader
leaf
leak*
lean
leap
learn
leather
leave
leaves*
left
leg
legend*
legendary*
leisure*
lemon
lemonade*
lend
length*
lens*
leopard
less
lesson (class)
let
letter
lettuce*
level*
lever*
liar*
librarian*
library
lick
lid
lie
life
lifeboat
lift
light
lighthouse
lightning

like
likely*
line
lion
lioness*
lip
lipstick*
liquid
listen
liter*
little
live
lively*
liver
lizard*
load*
lobster*
locomotive*
long
look
loose
lose
lot
loud
loudspeaker*
love
lovable
lovely*
low
lower*
luck*
lump
luxury*

M
machine
machine gun*
machinery*
mad*
made*
magic
magnet
magnetic*
magnify*
make
makeup*
male
mammal
mammoth*
man
mane*
many
map
marble*

March
march
mare*
margarine*
margin*
mark
market*
marmalade*
marriage*
marry
marsupial*
mascot*
mask
match
material
mathematics*
mattress*
May
meadow*
meal
mean
meaning*
measure
meat
mechanic*
mechanical*
medal*
medicine
meet
meeting*
melt
memory*
men*
mend
merry*
mess
message
messenger*
metal
method*
meter*
microphone*
microscope
middle
midnight
migrate*
military*
milk
million
millionaire*
mine*
miner*
mineral*
miniature*

minus*
minute
miracle*
mirage*
mirror
miser*
miserable*
miss
mistake
mix
mixer*
mixture*
moccasin*
modern*
moment*
Monday
money
monkey
monster*
month
moon
moonlight
moor*
more
morning
mosque
mosquito
moss*
most*
moth
motor*
mountain
mountaineer*
mouse
mouth
move
movement*
much
mud
multiply
murder*
muscle
museum
mushroom
music
musician*
mutter*
mystery*

N
nail
naked*
name
narrow

nasty*
nation*
national*
nationality*
natural*
nature
naught*
naughty
navigate*
navy*
near
nearly
neat
necessary*
neck
necklace*
need
needle
neglect*
neighbor
neighborhood*
neither
nephew
nerve*
nervous*
nest
net
netball*
never
new
news*
newspaper
next
niece
night
nightmare*
nobody
nod*
noise
noisy*
nomad*
none*
nonsense*
normal*
north
nose
nostril*
note*
nothing
notice
noun*
November
now
nowadays*

nowhere
number
nun*
nurse
nut
nylon*

O
oak
oar*
oasis
obedient*
obey*
object*
oblige*
observe*
occasion*
occupation*
occupy*
occur*
ocean
o'clock
October
octopus*
odd
offer
office*
often
oil
ointment*
old
old-fashioned
once*
onion
only
open
opening*
opposite
or
orange
orbit*
orchard*
orchestra*
order*
ordinary
organ*
original*
ornament*
orphan*
ostrich
other
out
outdoors*
outgrow*

outing*
outline*
outside
over
overcoat*
overhang*
overhead*
owe*
owl
own
owner*
ox*
oxen*
oxygen*

P
pack
package*
packet*
paddle*
page
pain
paint
painting*
pair
palace
pale*
palm
pan
pancake
panda
pants
paper
parachute
parade
parallel*
parcel
pardon*
parent
park
parliament
parrot
part
party
pass
passage*
passenger*
Passover
past
paste*
pastime*
pastry*
path
patience*

patient*
pattern
pause*
paw
pay
pea
peace
peach
peacock*
peanut
pear
pearl*
pebble
peculiar*
pedal
peel
peep
pen
pencil
penguin
peninsula*
penny*
people
pepper*
perch*
perfect*
perform*
performance*
perfume*
perhaps
period*
permission*
permit*
person
persuade*
pet
petal
pharaoh*
phone*
photograph
phrase*
physical*
physics*
piano
pick
picnic
picture
pie
piece
pig
pigeon*
piglet*
pigsty*
pile

pill
pillar*
pillow
pilot
pin
pinch*
pine*
pineappl
pink
pioneer*
pip*
pipe
pirate*
pit*
pitch
place
plain*
plait*
plan
plane*
planet
plant
plastic
plate
plateau*
platform
play
player*
playgrou
please
pleasant*
pleasure*
plenty*
plot*
plow
plug*
plum*
plunge*
plus*
pocket
poem
poet*
poetry*
point
poison
pole
police
polish
polite
pollen*
pollute*
pond
pony
pool

poor
pope*
popular
population
porch*
porcupine*
pork*
porpoise*
port*
possess*
possible*
poster*
pot
potato
pottery*
pound
pour
powder
power*
powerful
praise*
pray*
prayer*
precious*
prefer*
preferred*
prehistoric*
prepare*
present
president
press
pretend
pretty
prevent*
prey
price
prick*
priest*
primary*
prince
princess
print
prison
prisoner*
private*
prize
problem
produce*
producer*
product*
program
promise
proof*
propel*

propeller*
protect
proud
prove
provide*
prowl*
prune*
public*
publish*
pudding
puddle
pull
pulley*
pump*
pumpkin*
punch
punish
pupil
puppet
puppy
pure*
purple
purr*
purse
pursue*
push
put
puzzle

Q
quack
quality*
quantity*
quarrel
quarry*
quarter
quay*
queen
question
quick
quiet
quilt
quite
quiz

R
rabbi*
rabbit
race
radar*
radio
rag*
raid*
rail
rain
rainbow
raise
raisin*
rake*
rap*
rapid*
rare*
rat*
rattle
raw*
ray*
razor*
reach
read
ready
real
rebel*
receive*
recent*
recipe*
recite*
recognize*
record
recover*
rectangle*
red
refrigerator
rehearse*
rehearsal*
reign*
reindeer*
relative*
relax*
religion*

remain*
remainder*
remember
remind*
remove*
repair*
repeat*
replace*
reply
report*
reptile*
republic*
rescue
rest
restaurant
result*
return
revenge*
reverse*
revolution*
revolver*
reward*
rhinoceros
rhyme
rhythm*
ribbon
rice
rich
riddle*
ride
rider*
right
ring
rink*
rinse*
rip*
ripe
rise
risk*
river
road
roar
roast
rob
robber*

robe*
robot*
rock
rocket
rodeo*
roll
roller skate
roof
room
root
rope
rose
rotten*
rough
round
row
royal*
rubber*
ruby*
rudder*
rude*
rug
ruin*
rule
ruler*
run
rush*
rust*

S
sack*
sad
saddle
safe
sail
sailor
saint*
salad*
sale*
salt
salute*
same
sand
sandal
sandwich*
satellite*

satisfactory*
satisfied*
satisfy*
Saturday
sauce*
saucepan*
saucer*
sausage*
savage*
save
savings*
saw
scaffolding*
scald*
scar*
scarce*
scare*
scarf*
scarlet*
scene*
scenery*
scent*
school
science
scientist*
scissors
scooter*
scorch*
scout*
scratch
scream*
screen
screw
screwdriver*
scribble*
sculptor*
sculpture*
sea
sea gull*
seal
sea level*
search*
season
seat*
seaweed*
second
secret
secretary*
see
seed
seem*
seesaw*
seize*
seldom*

select*
self*
selfish*
sell
send
senior*
sense*
sensible*
sentence*
sentry*
separate*
September
sergeant*
serious*
servant*
serve*
set*
several*
severe*
sew
shadow
shake
shallow*
shame*
shampoo*
shape
share
shark*
sharp
shave*
she
shed*
sheep
sheepdog*
sheet*
shelf
shell
shellfish*
shelter*
shine
ship
shipwreck*
shirt
shiver*
shock*
shoe
shoot
shop
shore
short
shoulder
shout
show
shower*

shriek*
shrimp*
shrink*
shrub*
shudder*
shut
shutter*
shy*
sick
side
siege*
sign
signal*
signature*
silence*
silent*
silhouette*
silk*
silver
similar*
simple*
since*
sincere*
sing
single
sink
sip*
sister
sit
six
size
skate*
skeleton
skin
skirt
sky
slow
small
smash*
smell
smile
smoke
smooth
snail
snake
sneeze
snore*
snout*
snow
soak*
soap
sob*
soccer*
sock

Speller

sofa★
soft
soil★
soldier
sole★
solve★
somersault★
something
sometimes
somewhere★
son
song
soon★
sorrow★
sorry
sort★
sound
soup
sour
south
sow★
space
spacecraft★
spade★
spark★
sparkle★
sparrow★
speak
spear★
special
speck★
spectacles★
speech★
speed★
spell
spend
sphere★
spice★
spider
spill★
spin
spine★
spire★
spit★
splash
splendid★
splinter★
sponge★
spoon
sport★
spot
spread★
spring
spy★

square
squash★
squeeze★
squint★
squirrel
stable★
stadium★
stair
stale★
stalk★
stammer★
stamp★
stand
star
stare★
start
startle★
starve★
station
stationary★
(not moving)
stationery★
(paper, etc.)
stay★

steady★
steak★
steal
steam
steel★
stem
step
stew★
stick
stiff★
still★
stilts★
sting
stink★
stir★

stitch
stomach
stone
stop
store
storm
story
straight
straighten★
strange
stranger★
strap
straw★
stream★
street
stretch
stretcher★
string
stripe
stroke★
strong
struggle★
student★
study★

stuff★
stupid★
stutter★
style★
submarine
subtract
success★
suck★
sudden★
suffer★
sugar
suggest★
suit
suitable★
suitcase★

sum
summer
sun
Sunday
sunrise★
sunset★
sunshine★
supermarket
supper★
surface★
surgeon★
surgery★
surname★
surprise
surround★
swallow
swan
sweep
sweet
swift★
swim
swing
sword★
synagogue
syrup★

T
table
tadpole★
tail
take
tale★
talent★
talk
tall
tame
tank★
tape★
tape recorder★
tar★
tart★
task★
taste
tax★
taxi
tea
teach
teacher
team
tear
tease
telephone
telescope★
television

tell
temper★
temperature
tempt★
ten
tennis
tent
tentacle★
term★
terrible★
terrify★
territory★
terror★
test
text★
thank
the
theater
their★
then
there
thermometer
thick
thief★
thin
think
third★
thirsty
though★
thought★
thousand
thread
threaten★
three
throat
throne★
through
throw
thumb
thunder
Thursday
ticket
tide★
tidy
tie
tiger
tight★
timber★
time
tin★
tiny
tired
tissue
title★

toad★
toadstool★
toast★
today
toe
together
tomato
tomorrow
tongue
tonight
tool
tooth
toothbrush★
top
torch★
tortoise
torture★
toss★
total★
touch
tough★
towel
tower
town
toy
tractor
traffic
tragedy★
train
traitor★
transport★
trap★
travel
tray★
tread★
treasure
treat★
tree
tremble★
triangle
tribe★
tributary★
trick
tricycle★
trip★
trolley★
trot★
trouble★
truck
true
trumpet
trunk★
try
tub★

Tuesday
tunnel
turkey★
turn
turtle
twin
twinkle★
typewriter

U
ugly
umbrella
uncle
under
understand
undo★
unhappy
unicorn★
uniform
union★
unit★
unite★
universal★
universe★
university★
unknown★
unless★
untidy
until★
up
upset★
upside down
upstairs
urgent★
use
useful★
useless★
usual★
usually

V
vacant★
vacuum★
vain★
valley★
vanish
vase★
vast★
vegetable
vehicle
veil★
vein★
verb★

verse★
very
vessel★
vet★
vibrate★
victory★
view
village★
vinegar★
violin
visit
visitor★
vitamin★
voice
volcano
vote★
vowel★
vulture

W
wade★
wag★
wagon
waist
wait
wake
walk
wall
walrus★
wander★
want
war
warm
warn★
warning★
wash
wasp★
waste
watch
water
waterfall★
waterproof★
wave
wax★
weak
wealth★
wealthy★
weapon★
wear
weather
Wednesday
week
weigh
welcome★

well	while★	widow★	wine★	wolf	worm	**X**	yearly★	young
west	whip★	widower★	wing	wolves	worry★	X ray	yeast★	
wet	whisker★	wife	wink★	woman	worth★	xylophone	yell★	**Z**
whale	whisper	wig★	winter	wonderful★	wrap		yellow	zebra
what	whistle	wigwam★	wipe	wood	wreck★	**Y**	yesterday	zero
wheat	white	wild	wire	wooden★	wrestle★	yacht	yet★	zigzag
wheel	who	win	wish	wool	wrist	yak★	Yiddish★	zipper
wheelbarrow★	whole	wind	witch	woolen★	write	yard	yoga★	zone★
when	why	windmill★	with	word	writing★	yarn★	yogurt	zoo
where	wicked★	windshield★	without★	work	written★	yawn	yoke★	
which	wide	window	wizard	world	wrong	year	yolk	

Our Earth in Space

The earth we live on is called a *planet*. It spins around and around in space. As it spins it travels around the sun. There are eight other planets traveling around the sun. The sun is a giant ball of hot gas. It gives light and heat to the earth. The sun is a *star*. There are millions of other stars in the universe. You can see stars on a clear, cloudless night twinkling in the sky.

The earth has one moon. It travels around the earth. It takes four weeks to do so – a month. The moon is 238,900 miles away from the earth. On July 20, 1969, two American astronauts became the first people to walk on the moon.

Our planet is the only one with sea. Around the earth is a layer of air. This is called the *atmosphere*. All living things need water and air to survive. The earth is the only planet we know of which has life.

More of the earth is covered by water than by land. The large areas of water are *oceans*.

The land on the earth is divided into seven parts. These are called *continents*. They are Europe, Asia, Africa, North America, South America, Australasia, and Antarctica. All the continents, except Antarctica, are divided into *countries*. If you look on the next two pages you will see a map of all the countries of the world.

Countries of the World

Greenland

ICELAND

Alaska (USA)

CANADA

UNITED STATES OF AMERICA

TROPIC OF CANCER

MEXICO

BAHAMAS

CUBA

46
53
48
50
54 55
47
52
49 51

PUERTO RICO
DOMINICA
ST LUCIA

56
57

VENEZUELA

COLOMBIA

58
59 60

EQUATOR

ECUADOR

PERU

BRAZIL

BOLIVIA

PARAGUAY

TROPIC OF CAPRICORN

URUGUAY

ARGENTINA

Falkland Islands

IRELAND

UNITED KINGD

FRA
7

PORTUGAL

SPAIN

MOROCCO

25

WESTERN SAHARA

ALGE

MAURITANIA

MAL

CAPE VERDE ISLANDS

26
27
28
29
30
31
32

IVORY COAST
GHANA

33
3

1 DENMARK	11 YUGOSLAVIA
2 NETHERLANDS	12 ALBANIA
3 BELGIUM	13 CYPRUS
4 LUXEMBOURG	14 LEBANON
5 W. GERMANY	15 ISRAEL
6 E. GERMANY	16 SYRIA
7 SWITZERLAND	17 JORDAN
8 AUSTRIA	18 KUWAIT
9 CZECHOSLOVAKIA	19 BAHRAIN
10 HUNGARY	20 UNITED ARAB EMIRATES

FINLAND

U S S R

LAND

10 ROMANIA
11 BULGARIA
12
GREECE
TURKEY
13 16
15
14
IRAQ   IRAN
17
BYA
EGYPT   18 19
SAUDI
ARABIA   20
OMAN

MONGOLIA

NORTH
KOREA
CHINA   JAPAN
SOUTH
KOREA

AFGHAN-
ISTAN
PAKISTAN   NEPAL   22

23   BURMA   LAOS   TAIWAN
INDIA   Hong Kong
21 YEMEN P.D.R.
41   THAILAND   VIETNAM   PHILIPPINES
SOMALI   24
HAD   REPUBLIC
SUDAN   SRI LANKA   BRUNEI
34   ETHIOPIA   MALDIVES   MALAYSIA
39 38   INDONESIA   SINGAPORE
KENYA   SEYCHELLES   PAPUA   SOLOMON
ZAIRE   NEW   ISLANDS
40 TANZANIA   GUINEA
42 COMOROS
GOLA   VANUATU
ZAMBIA   MOZAMBIQUE   MADAGASCAR   MAURITIUS   FIJI
43   NEW
BOTSWANA   CALEDONIA
MBIA
SOUTH   44   AUSTRALIA
AFRICA
45

NEW
ZEALAND

21 YEMEN	31 LIBERIA	41 DJIBOUTI	51 COSTA RICA
22 BHUTAN	32 BURKINA FASO	42 MALAWI	52 PANAMA
23 BANGLADESH	33 TOGO	43 ZIMBABWE	53 JAMAICA
24 KAMPUCHEA	34 CENTRAL AFRICAN REPUBLIC	44 SWAZILAND	54 HAITI
25 TUNISIA	35 EQUATORIAL GUINEA	45 LESOTHO	55 DOMINICAN REPUBLIC
26 SENEGAL	36 GABON	46 BELIZE	56 BARBADOS
27 GAMBIA	37 CAMEROON	47 GUATEMALA	57 TRINIDAD AND TOBAGO
28 GUINEA-BISSAU	38 UGANDA	48 HONDURAS	58 GUYANA
29 GUINEA	39 RWANDA	49 EL SALVADOR	59 SURINAM
30 SIERRA LEONE	40 BURUNDI	50 NICARAGUA	60 FRENCH GUIANA

The English language was first spoken in England, which is one of the areas of the British Isles. The map opposite shows the two separate nations that make up the British Isles. They are the Republic of Ireland and the United Kingdom of Great Britain and Northern Ireland. Great Britain is made up of three countries – England, Scotland, and Wales. London is the capital of the United Kingdom.

Until 1714 Scotland was a separate country with its own parliament. Today Scotland still has some different laws from England and Wales. It also has its own system of education and its own national church – the Church of Scotland. Most Scottish people speak English. Gaelic is still spoken in some parts of the country. The capital of Scotland is Edinburgh.

Wales was conquered by England in the 1200s. Nearly everyone can speak English but Welsh is also spoken by more than a quarter of a million people. The capital is Cardiff.

When the south of Ireland became independent in 1921, Northern Ireland remained a part of the United Kingdom. Its capital is Belfast.

The Republic of Ireland has a population of three and a half million. One hundred and fifty years ago twice as many people lived there as do today. After the Great Famine of the 1840s many people moved to other countries to find work. The capital of Ireland is Dublin. Most people speak English, but Irish, one of the Celtic languages, is also a national language.

The map on the opposite page shows the main towns, ports, and rivers of the British Isles. The illustrations on the map show the main things that people do to earn a living.

There are many towns with lots of factories in the middle and the north of England, also in the middle of Scotland, in South Wales and in Northern Ireland. These are the areas where coal is found. Once coal was the most important fuel, but now oil and gas from under the North Sea are used as well. Ireland is mainly a farming country.

Although the British Isles are small, they contain many different kinds of scenery. In Wales, Scotland, and the north of England there are mountains. The highest mountain is Ben Nevis in Scotland. Can you find it on the map? The west of Britain gets the most rain and a lot of land is used for animal farming. The land in the south and in the east is flatter and drier, so farmers can grow wheat and barley. Ireland is a green and beautiful country. It often rains there, so animal farming is very important.

United Kingdom

Ireland

ORKNEY ISLANDS

John o' Groats

SHETLAND ISLANDS

HEBRIDES

Inverness

Loch Ness

Dee

Ben Nevis

Aberdeen

Grampians

Perth

Dundee

SCOTLAND

ATLANTIC OCEAN

Glasgow

Edinburgh

NORTH SEA

N
W E
S

Tyne

Londonderry

Newcastle

Belfast

Lake District

NORTHERN IRELAND

ISLE OF MAN

York

Hull

GREAT BRITAIN

REPUBLIC OF IRELAND (EIRE)

Halifax

Manchester

Leeds

Dublin

Liverpool

Sheffield

Shannon

IRISH SEA

Nottingham

Trent

Norwich

Cork

Birmingham

ENGLAND

Cambridge

WALES

Severn

Oxford

Swansea

Thames

Cardiff

Bristol

Bath

London

Dover

Southampton

Portsmouth

ISLE OF WIGHT

Plymouth

ISLES OF SCILLY

Land's End

ENGLISH CHANNEL

FRANCE

0 20 40 60 80 100 Kilometers

0 25 50 Miles

The United States of America

Just about every language in the world is spoken in the United States of America. But English is the official language. That so many languages are spoken is not really surprising. Over 83 percent of the country's population of 226,505,000 are descended from European immigrants (people who came from overseas). Black Americans form about 12 percent of the population.

The United States is the fourth largest country in the world in both area and population. The mainland area is divided into 48 states. Alaska, the forty-ninth state lies to the north-west of Canada. The fiftieth state is Hawaii, 312 islands in the Pacific Ocean.

Native Americans (Indians) lived in the country before the Europeans and other people came. The first colonists lived on the Atlantic coast to the east of the Appalachian Mountains. Gradually people started farming the flat plains of the "interior." Travelers and miners traveled west through the Rocky Mountains before reaching the Pacific coast.

The U.S.A. is today a rich and powerful nation.

America's capital city is Washington, D.C. Here the Congress meets and the President lives. The country's largest city is New York. The highest point is Mount McKinley in Alaska.

The country's motto is: "Out of many, one people". The flag is known by most people as the Stars and Stripes and the national anthem is called "The Star-Spangled Banner."

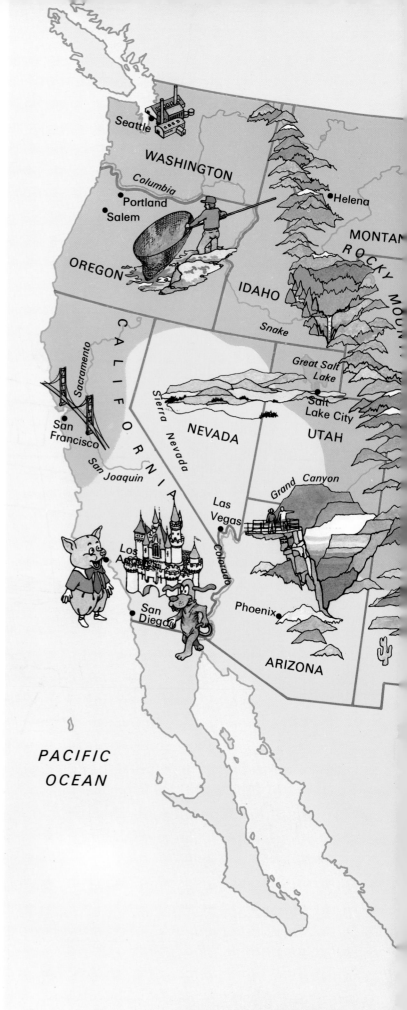

194

CANADA

NORTH DAKOTA

Missouri

Bismarck

MINNESOTA

Lake Superior

MICHIGAN

MAINE

VERMONT

N.H.

SOUTH DAKOTA

Pierre

Minneapolis

St. Paul

WISCONSIN

Lake Huron

Lake Michigan

Lake Ontario

Buffalo

NEW YORK

MASS.

CONN

RH IS

Boston

WYOMING

NEBRASKA

Omaha

IOWA

Des Moines

Mississippi

Milwaukee

Chicago

Detroit

Lake Erie

Cleveland

Pittsburgh

PENNSYLVANIA

New York City

N.J.

Philadelphia

DEL

Cheyenne

COLORADO

Denver

Arkansas

KANSAS

Kansas City

INDIANA

Indianapolis

OHIO

Cincinnati

WEST VIRGINIA

Ohio

Appalachian Mountains

Baltimore

Washington D.C.

Richmond

VIRGINIA

MA

Santa Fe

NEW MEXICO

OKLAHOMA

Oklahoma City

Red

Dallas

MISSOURI

St. Louis

ILLINOIS

KENTUCKY

Nashville

TENNESSEE

Tennessee

NORTH CAROLINA

SOUTH CAROLINA

Atlanta

Savannah

TEXAS

Little Rock

ARKANSAS

Memphis

Mississippi

Jackson

MISSISSIPPI

ALABAMA

Montgomery

GEORGIA

ATLANTIC OCEAN

Houston

San Antonio

Rio Grande

LOUISIANA

New Orleans

FLORIDA

Tampa

Miami

MEXICO

Kilometers
0   100 200 300 400 500
Miles 0   100   200   300

N
W   E
S

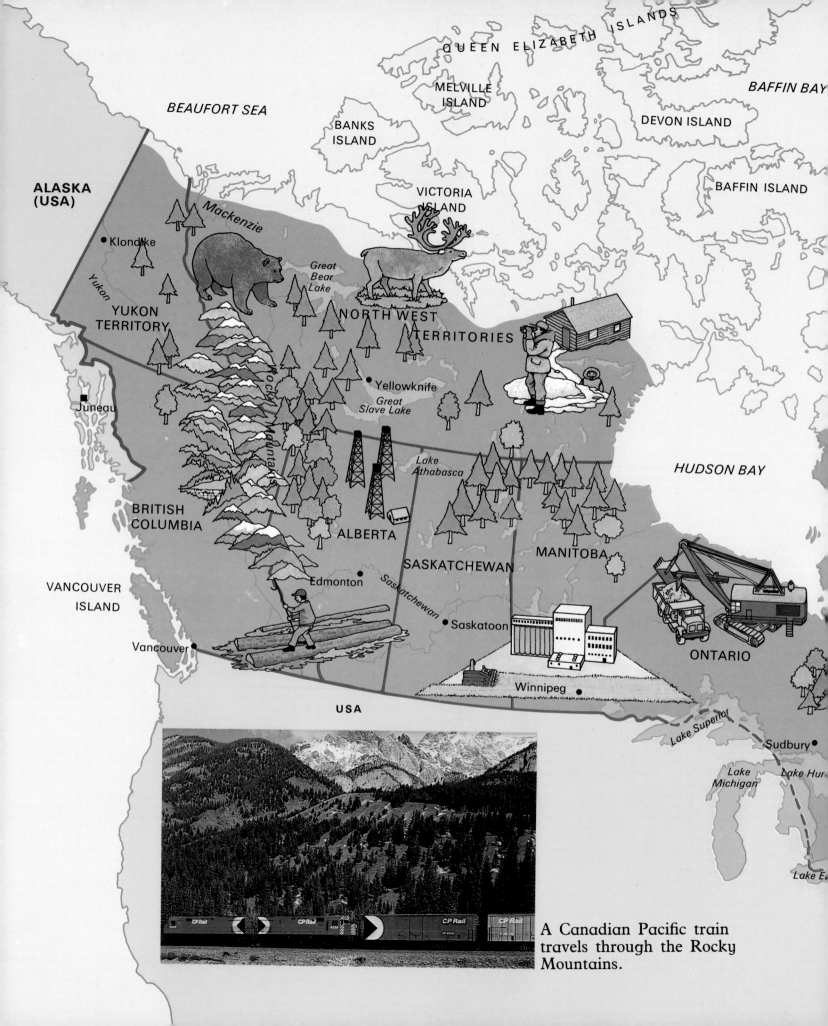

BEAUFORT SEA

QUEEN ELIZABETH ISLANDS

MELVILLE ISLAND

BANKS ISLAND

DEVON ISLAND

BAFFIN BAY

BAFFIN ISLAND

ALASKA (USA)

Mackenzie

Klondike

Yukon

YUKON TERRITORY

VICTORIA ISLAND

Great Bear Lake

NORTH WEST TERRITORIES

Juneau

Yellowknife

Great Slave Lake

HUDSON BAY

Lake Athabasca

BRITISH COLUMBIA

Rocky Mountains

ALBERTA

SASKATCHEWAN

MANITOBA

VANCOUVER ISLAND

Edmonton

Saskatchewan

ONTARIO

Vancouver

Saskatoon

Winnipeg

USA

Lake Superior

Sudbury

Lake Michigan

Lake Huron

Lake E.

A Canadian Pacific train travels through the Rocky Mountains.

Canada

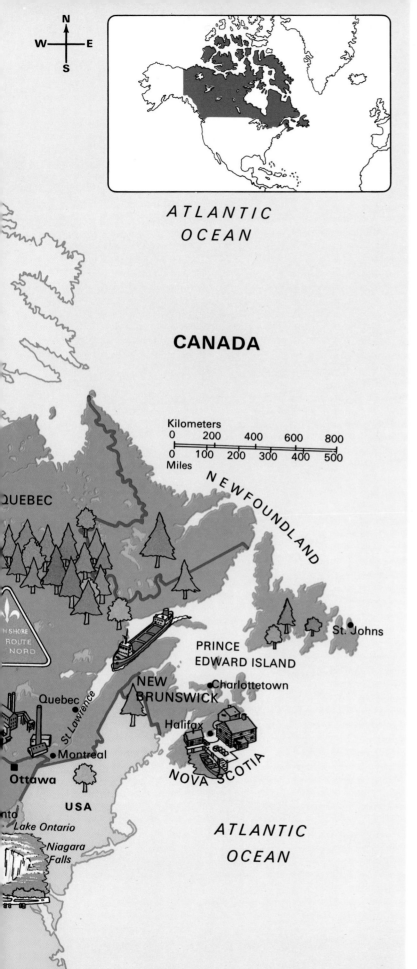

ATLANTIC
OCEAN

CANADA

Kilometers
0   200   400   600   800
0 100 200 300 400 500
Miles

NEWFOUNDLAND

QUEBEC

H SHORE
ROUTE
NORD

St. Johns

PRINCE
EDWARD ISLAND

NEW
BRUNSWICK

Charlottetown

Quebec

St. Lawrence

Halifax

NOVA SCOTIA

Montreal

Ottawa

USA

nto
Lake Ontario

Niagara
Falls

ATLANTIC
OCEAN

Canada has two official languages – English and French. The province of Quebec is the main French-speaking area of the country. Of all the countries in the world only the Soviet Union is bigger than Canada, yet there are fewer than 25 million Canadians. American Indians, Eskimos, and Aleuts were the first-known inhabitants of Canada. Today nearly half the people that live there are of British origin. A third are descended from French settlers. Most of the population lives in the south of the country, within about 120 miles of the United States border.

Canada has many different kinds of land. The great central plains are given over to pasture land and wheat farming. Farther east are the Great Lakes, five huge inland seas that empty into the St. Lawrence River. The great cities of Toronto and Montreal are found here.

The capital of Canada is Ottawa, where Parliament sits. Canada is a member of the Commonwealth and Queen Elizabeth II is also Queen of Canada.

197

Our World
Australia
& New Zealand

AUSTRALIA
Population   15 million
Capital   Canberra
Largest town   Sydney

NEW ZEALAND
Population   3,400,000
Capital   Wellington
Largest town   Auckland

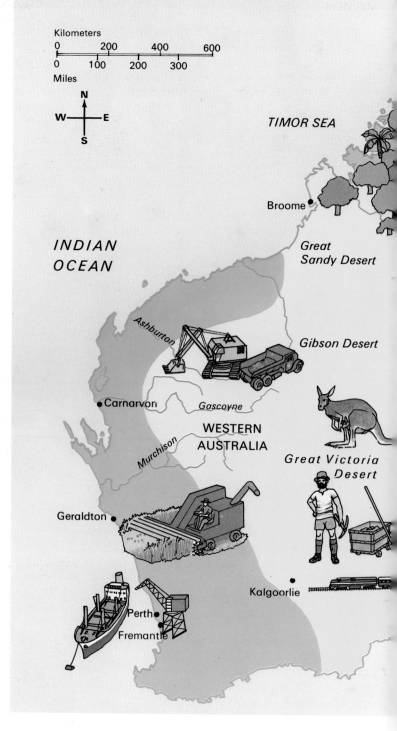

Kilometers
0   200   400   600
0   100   200   300
Miles

TIMOR SEA

Broome

INDIAN
OCEAN

Great
Sandy Desert

Ashburton

Gibson Desert

Carnarvon   Gascoyne

WESTERN
AUSTRALIA

Murchison

Great Victoria
Desert

Geraldton

Kalgoorlie

Perth

Fremantle

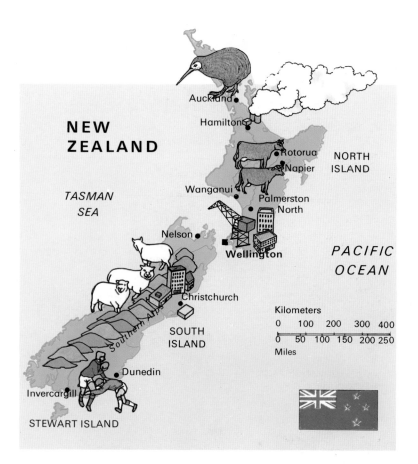

NEW
ZEALAND

Auckland

Hamilton

Rotorua

Napier

NORTH
ISLAND

TASMAN
SEA

Wanganui

Palmerston
North

Nelson

Wellington

PACIFIC
OCEAN

Christchurch

Southern Alps

SOUTH
ISLAND

Kilometers
0   100   200   300   400
0   50   100   150   200   250
Miles

Dunedin

Invercargill

STEWART ISLAND

ARAFURA SEA

MELVILLE ISLAND

Darwin

Ord

Victoria

NORTHERN TERRITORY

AUSTRALIA

Macdonnell Range

Ayers Rock

Musgrave Ranges

Nullarbor Plain

T AUSTRALIAN BIGHT

SOUTH AUSTRALIA

Lake Eyre

Lake Torrens

Whyalla

Adelaide

KANGAROO ISLAND

GULF OF CARPENTARIA

Cape York Peninsula

Groote Eylandt

WELLESLEY ISLAND

Leichhardt

Flinders

Mount Isa

QUEENSLAND

Georgina

Diamantina

Alice Springs

Simpson Desert

Cooper

Cairns

Townsville

Rockhampton

GREAT BARRIER REEF

PACIFIC OCEAN

Great Dividing Range

Brisbane

Broken Hill

Darling

NEW SOUTH WALES

Murray

Murrumbidgee

Newcastle

Sydney

Wollongong

Wagga Wagga

Canberra

VICTORIA

Australian Alps

TASMAN SEA

Ballarat

Geelong

Melbourne

KING ISLAND

FLINDERS ISLAND

Launceston

Hobart

TASMANIA